D0466275

# AMERICAN FOODWAYS

## What, When, Why and How We Eat In America

## CHARLES CAMP

This volume is part of
The American Folklore Series
W.K. McNeil, General Editor

**AUGUST HOUSE / LITTLE ROCK**

P U B L I S H E R S

© Copyright 1989 by Charles Camp
All rights reserved. This book, or parts thereof,
may not be reproduced in any form without permission.
Published by August House, Inc.,
P.O. Box 3223, Little Rock, Arkansas, 72203,
501-663-7300.

Printed in the United States of America

10 9 8 7 6 5 4 3 2 1

LIBRARY OF CONGRESS CATALOGING-IN-PUBLICATION DATA

Camp, Charles.
American foodways / edited by Charles Camp. – 1st ed.
p. cm. – (The American folklore series)
Bibliography: p.
ISBN 0-87483-096-6 (alk. paper): $19.95
1. Food habits–United States.
2. United States–Social life and customs.
I. Title. II. Series.
TX357.C257 1989
394.1'2'0973–dc20
89-33486
CIP

First Edition, 1989

Woodcut reproductions are taken from Joseph Crawhall,
*Quaint Cuts in the Chap Book Style* (Dover Publications, 1974).
Used by permission.
Typography by Lettergraphics, Memphis, Tennessee
Design direction by Suzanne Kittrell
Project direction by Hope Coulter

This book is printed on archival-quality paper which meets the
guidelines for performance and durability of the Committee on
Production Guidelines for Book Longevity of the Council on
Library Resources.

AUGUST HOUSE, INC.                    PUBLISHERS                    LITTLE ROCK

This book is dedicated
to families, who carry the weight of tradition,
and children, who lighten it.

# CONTENTS

## ACKNOWLEDGMENTS

I want to thank all the people who encouraged me and contributed their suggestions and criticisms to this work—Dan Buck, Bill Ivey, Tim Lloyd, Nan Martin-Perdue, Bill McNeil, Kathy Neustadt, Mark Neustadt, Chuck Perdue, Sue Samuelson, Betty Stark, Shalom Staub, Bob Teske, Don Yoder, the members of the American Folklore Society Foodways Section, and especially my wife, Andrea, and my children, Dana and Nick.

Among the institutions that provided hospitality and resources were the Agricultural Experimental Station of Mississippi State University, Johns Hopkins University, the Manuscript Division of the Library of Congress, the National Agriculture Library, the National Research Council, the Schlesinger Library of Harvard University, and the Smithsonian Institution's Office of Folklife Programs.

# INTRODUCTION

The initial interest of folklorists in the study of American foodways was stimulated by an ancillary concern with the folklore of minority groups. The first folklorist to write at length on traditional foods was the peripatetic Lafcadio Hearn (1850–1904), a writer now best remembered for his interest in things Japanese. A native of the Ionian Island of Santa Maura, Hearn spent his boyhood in Ireland and England and later moved to the United States, the West Indies, and finally to Japan. Besides traveling a lot Hearn was, by his own admission, a person who worshipped the odd, the queer, the strange, the exotic, and the monstrous.[1] This feature of his personality inclined him towards the study of the offbeat and non-standard, which in turn led him to the investigation of minority cultures. While his primary folklore interests were in the areas of folksong and legendry, he also found foodways particularly appealing, demonstrating this interest with a book, *La Cuisine Creole* (1885), whose title page lists William H. Coleman as author. Apparently, Hearn gathered the recipes between 1877 and 1884, when he was in New Orleans. Two years after the publication of *La Cuisine Creole* he left Louisiana and eventually settled in Japan, but he never lost his interest in foodways. While in Martinique, in the West Indies, he wrote about holiday dishes of the poor—possum caterpillar, sausages, and chicken with rice—which he compared to Louisiana Creole delicacies. After moving to Japan he was surprised to find the Nipponese as fond of rice as the West Indians, but their manner of preparing it was distasteful to him, and he wrote his friends apologizing for his inability to exist on Japanese fare.[2]

Possibly, as F.A. de Caro suggests, Hearn didn't consider his collection of Creole recipes a contribution to folklore; the pseudonymous publication implies as much. Nevertheless, he had previously indicated in several newspaper columns that he planned to edit a cookbook.[3] *La Cuisine Creole* is a collection that got relatively little attention at the time, being among the least used of Hearn's several books. Despite its relative lack of influence the little volume is not unimportant. It is significant not only because of its early date but also because of its discussion of nineteenth-century New Orleans ethnocuisine, its traditional recipes, and its "household hints." *La Cuisine Creole* also includes some proverbs, street cries, and woodcuts of New Orleans street life, by this means providing something of the traditional context within which the cookery flourished.

*Hearn was, by his own admission, a person who worshipped the odd, the queer, the strange, the exotic, and the monstrous. This feature of his personality inclined him towards the study of the offbeat and non-standard, which in turn led him to the investigation of minority cultures. While his primary folklore interests were in the areas of folksong and legendry, he also found foodways particularly appealing.*

Far more attention in the late nineteenth century was accorded to the second publication on foodways by an American folklorist. Although this was an article rather than a book, it gained more notice in scholarly circles for a variety of reasons. First, unlike Hearn, who was considered an eccentric by many, the author, John G. Bourke (1843–1896), was a highly respected scholar who was to become president of the American Folklore Society. Second, the essay, "The Folk Foods of the Rio Grande Valley and of Northern Mexico," appeared in the most reputable folklore journal of the time, the *Journal of American Folklore.*[4] Third, Bourke's article was more clearly tied to evolutionary doctrines popular at the time than was Hearn's book. Fourth, this essay, and Bourke's other publications on Mexican-American culture, were produced with a very specific immediate application in mind. A professional soldier, Bourke considered accurate information about food traditions useful in preparing the soldiers for their hostile surroundings. He reflected that "it might perhaps happen that an officer would find himself beleaguered, and supply trains cut off, in which case there would be no alternative of surrender or retreat, unless he could provide food for his troops from the resources of the country."[5] At the same time, Bourke maintained, knowing about traditional foods and customs could help "improve" Mexican culture, by which he meant destroy it. Like other evolutionists of his time, Bourke was convinced there was a natural progression of society from savagery to civilization, the only fully desirable plateau. His various prejudices about progress and regression shaped by his evolutionist dogma led him to the opinion that there was only one legitimate reason to study foodways, or any other aspect of traditional culture: a knowledge of such material would facilitate the task of abolishing the "savage" stage of culture represented by such traditions. His evolutionary stance also led him to concern himself primarily with survivals of "savage" foods.

Bourke's theoretical prejudices notwithstanding, his article is still useful, as is to a lesser degree a subsequent one, "Notes on the Language and Folk Usage of the Rio Grande Valley" which, despite its title, deals with, among other things, traditional foods.[6] Indeed, in some respects this essay is quite modern. A number of dishes are discussed, with attention given to regional variation and historical origins of cooking practices and plant cultivation. Bourke's annotations are frequently extensive and always worthwhile. He resorts to all types of sources in his search for parallels. The stove used by traditional cooks along the Texas border is found to be the same as that generally utilized by the ancient Romans.[7] Throughout the article writers ranging from Madame Calderon de la Barco to Francis Parkman, government documents, and various other references are used to demonstrate the ancestry and lineage of Texas foodways. Equally important are the glimpses Bourke provides of his fieldwork and of some of the informants who contributed data for his notebooks. A Señora Ornelas he met in Camargo seemed particularly memorable to Bourke. Although he emphasized a distaste for garlic, she insisted upon including it with every meal. She cut short his complaints by remarking that "one must have garlic."[8] Equally unforgettable was a *nevero* (ice-cream man) in Monterey whose pleas were so persuasive that he conned several people, including Bourke, into purchasing his wares even though a cold north wind was blowing.

Despite the generally good reception of Bourke's article and the influence of its author, the essay was not followed by any flowering of folklore studies of American foodways. In fact, one of the trends of American foodways scholarship is a period of great activity followed by a lull of studies. For fifty years "The Folk-Foods of the Rio Grande Valley and of Northern Mexico" remained the only discussion of traditional foods in the *Journal of American Folklore.* Then, in 1945, Norman D. Humphrey's "Some Dietary and Health Practices of Detroit Mexicans" became the second article on foodways to appear in the august journal, but Humphrey's remarks were far less extensive than Bourke's.[9] The subject of Mexican-American foodways has received most attention in the Publications of the Texas Folklore Society, but most of these articles have been very brief, rambling discussions that are nevertheless useful because they usually include anecdotes that reveal much about traditional foodways.[10] Some, such as Ruth Dodson's paper "Tortilla Making," are detailed descriptions of specialized aspects of folk cookery.[11] Others, such as Bill Tate's *Truchas . . . Village with a View: Life in a Spanish Village* (1969), have information about regional dishes thrown in almost as an afterthought.[12] There have been relatively few works like Alicia Gonzalez's "'Guess How Doughnuts Are Made': Verbal and Nonverbal Aspects of the *Pandero* and His Stereotype," which is based on a relatively large number of field interviews.[13] Whatever the approach, none of these publications owes much to Bourke; in most instances romanticism or nostalgia was the motivating factor behind them.

Although neither Hearn nor Bourke stimulated immediate subsequent research in American foodways, the two men did succeed in establishing the two basic approaches to treating traditional cookery and its lore that most subsequent folklorists dealing with the topic followed, namely the anecdotal collection of recipes or the collection of food as a folklore genre. Of these, the former has, until recently, been the most commonly used. Occasionally there appeared a publication like Susan F. Rogers's brief "Colonial Cookery Terms," which belonged in neither camp, but such collections have been rare.[14]

*During the first seven decades of the twentieth century, a surprisingly large number of volumes appeared that are essentially recipe collections aimed at a popular audience but are nonetheless valuable to foodways scholars because of numerous pertinent yarns and anecdotes they contain.*

During the first seven decades of the twentieth century, a surprisingly large number of volumes appeared that are essentially recipe collections aimed at a popular audience but are nonetheless valuable to foodways scholars because of numerous pertinent yarns and anecdotes they contain. Volumes such as Imogen B. Wolcott's *The Yankee Cook Book* (1939) and *The American Heritage Cookbook and Illustrated History of American Eating and Drinking* (1964) are liberally sprinkled with anecdotes taken from historical and contemporary sources. To a certain extent their anecdotal nature is the main value of works such as Sheila Hibben's *American Regional Cookery* (1946), Euell Gibbon's *Stalking the Blue-Eyed Scallop* (1964), Dale Brown's *American Cooking* (1968), and Esther Aresty's *The Delectable Past* (1969), all of which are purportedly more than recipe collections but none of which is theoretical or written from a folklore viewpoint. There have also been several attempts at producing a general history of American dietary habits, of which the most important remains Richard Osborn Cummings's *The American and His Food: A History of Food Habits in the United States* (1940). Three more recent books, Waverley Root and Richard de Rochemont's *Eating in America* (1976), Richard J. Hooker's *A History of Food and Drink in America* (1981), and Kathryn Grover's *Dining in America 1850–1900* (1987), are valuable reading, but in all of them the folklore viewpoint receives at best only incidental consideration.

Prior to the 1970s the bulk of comments on foodways that appeared in folklore journals were in survey articles concerned with the lore of specific groups. An example is Agnes Nolan Underwood's "Folklore from G.I. Joe," which deals with several genres, including food.[15] Benjamin A. Botkin included sections on regional foods in some of his folklore "treasuries," but the material is presented with little or no comment and some of it is not folk. A significant body of reliable material was gathered by the fieldworkers for the WPA during the 1930s and 1940s, but most of that data is unpublished and largely inaccessible. Thus, while some folklorists have been interested in food and its traditions for over a century, most of this attention has been incidental and not the result of an intensive study of foodways. It is hardly surprising, then, that the work done prior to 1970 went in spurts and that none of it stimulated any extensive investigations of food traditions by Americans interested in folk culture.

An important date in the history of American foodways studies is 1970, for in that year Don Yoder, who would become the most influential folklorist involved with this area of study, attended the first International Symposium on Ethnological Food Research held in Lund, Sweden. That same year Nils-Arvid Bringeus, organizer of the Lund conference, published *Mat och Miljo* (Food and Milieu), a book that had come to Yoder's attention primarily through a translation of one chapter in the Welsh journal *Folk Life.*[16] Bringeus argued for studies of the relationship between culture, food, and environment and was particularly interested in what he termed "food and fellowship." He maintained that eating habits reveal "lines of demarcation between the classes of a community" and at the same time "serve as links between people."[17]

Yoder found the conference stimulating and it bolstered his longstanding interest in foodways. In the early 1960s he had produced three fine, detailed studies of Pennsylvania-German folk foods, treating them from a historical and comparative nature much as folktale specialists discussed traditional narratives.[18] In 1972 Yoder's article on "Folk Cookery" appeared in Richard M. Dorson's textbook *Folklore and Folklife: An Introduction.*[19] This twenty-five–page essay has been lauded as "the first clear 'call to arms' for an intensive study of foodways by Americans interested in folk culture."[20] There is considerable truth to this statement, for although a number of prior American folklorists had treated the subject, none influenced subsequent research as much as Yoder and none outlined the possibilities for research that he did. Of course, this listing of future prospects was virtually required because the article appeared in a textbook; its issuance in this context also increased the likelihood that the essay would be influential.

Because this seminal essay was so significant in American foodways scholarship, a closer look at its contents is merited. The paper consists of five parts: food in folk culture, research problems in American folk cookery, the function of folk cookery, folk cookery and material culture, and traditional cookery in the twentieth century. Yoder notes that it "is to the European studies that we must look for guidance."[21] He further suggests two major directions that students of American traditional cookery should follow: regional variations in domestic cookery and "the comparative study of the relation of American to European folk patterns of cookery."[22] Yoder sees an urgency for folklore research on foodways because regional cookery is declining, being replaced by an eclectic "American" cookery that rises above regionality. There are, however, relict areas "where earlier foodways have been preserved in the face of contemporary social change."[23] Appalachia, which contains elements from several areas, is, in Yoder's view, the most important of these relict areas. He also finds the study of meal systems in specific folk cultures especially fruitful, as are the investigation of areas, such as folk religion and material culture, "into which folk cookery ramifies."[24] He then provides several examples of how religious and material culture and foodways intersect. Finally, Yoder attempts to sum up the meaning of traditional cookery in contemporary society. Ultimately, the study of folk cookery is viewed as a complex area of scholarship that "includes the study of the foods themselves, their morphology, their preparation, their preservation, their social and psychological functions, and their ramifications into all other aspects of folk culture."[25]

Thus, Yoder saw foodways research as basically historical and descriptive. Indeed, since he believed traditional cookery was disappearing, studies of the past or relict areas were the only fruitful type of food studies possible. Foodways scholarship, then, was basically an exercise in cultural archaeology, and those who studied the topic were essentially dealing with survivals. In other words, Yoder adopted essentially the same attitude early ballad and folktale collectors evinced towards their subject. His viewpoint was accepted by most foodways scholars at the time, but there were some exceptions. A year previously, in 1971, Jay Anderson, one of Yoder's students, had suggested that the historical and regional emphasis was important but future research should be based on the "conceptual model." This term Anderson understood to refer "to the whole interrelated *system* of food conceptualization and evaluation, procurement, distribution, preservation, preparation, consumption, and nutrition shared by all the members of a particular society."[26]

Anderson's view of food as not only an item but also as a means of expression and communication between people was bolstered by other essays that appeared in the same jour-

*Bringeus argued for studies of the relationship between culture, food, and environment and was particularly interested in what he termed "food and fellowship." He maintained that eating habits reveal "lines of demarcation between the classes of a community" and at the same time "serve as links between people."*

*Yoder's article on "Folk Cookery" has been lauded as "the first clear 'call to arms' for an intensive study of foodways by Americans interested in folk culture." The paper consists of five parts: food in folk culture, research problems in American folk cookery, the function of folk cookery, folk cookery and material culture, and traditional cookery in the twentieth century. Yoder sees an urgency for folklore research on foodways because regional cookery is declining, being replaced by an eclectic "American" cookery that rises above regionality.*

nal issue as his paper.[27] The immediate response to Anderson's article and its companions and to Yoder's essay was not increased foodways studies but, rather, a temporary silence on the subject. In the late 1970s, perhaps in response to works by anthropologists, most notably Mary Douglas, who discussed food as an art form, much new work on foodways was undertaken by folklorists. In response to this renewed interest the Foodways Section of the American Folklore Society established, in conjunction with the University of Pennsylvania's Department of Folklore and Folklife, a newsletter titled *The Digest: A Newsletter for the Interdisciplinary Study of Food* (1977). At the same time Charles Camp was conducting research for his Ph.D. dissertation that focused on the America Eats program of the Works Progress Administration (WPA). This work and subsequent articles based on it are important because they suggested a basic reorientation of thinking about foodways studies.[28] Camp proposed that folklorists investigating food traditions would be best served by emphasizing events rather than the food itself.

The argument of Camp's dissertation was supported by subsequent scholars. In an 1979 article in the *Journal of the Folklore Institute,* Lin T. Humphrey agreed there was a need to know how people use food as a means of bringing about social interaction. Her categorization of picnics, potlucks, cocktail parties, box socials, and the like as small group festive gatherings was a refinement of Camp's term, food events. In offering a typology of these events and in demonstrating how community and festival scholarship could be combined with folklore approaches to the study of food traditions to create a new method of foodways research, Humphrey went beyond Camp.

Most of the scholars active in the 1970s and 1980s agreed that an interdisciplinary approach to the study of foodways was desirable. Even so, it was not until the 1980s that any books were published that espoused this viewpoint. Then, four volumes either explicitly or implicitly made this argument. First among these was *Foodways and Eating Habits: Directions for Research* (1983) which first appeared as a special issue of *Western Folklore*—only the second time an American folklore journal has been entirely devoted to the subject of foodways.[29] Editors Michael Owen Jones, Bruce Giuliano, and Roberta Krell presented thirteen papers by folklorists, historians, experimental psychologists, and consumer research specialists who sought "to combine approaches in the arts, humanities, and social sciences in order to enhance the understanding of human behavior." Jones, Giuliano, and Krell found the interdisciplinary approach essential because "the matter of procuring and consuming foods is fundamental to our lives, not only for survival but also as it concerns our conceptions of ourselves and our perceptions of the natural and social environments. . . . Preparing, serving, and eating food often provide a basis for interaction, serve as a vehicle of communication, and constitute a source of associations and symbolic structures."[30]

*Foodways and Eating Habits* was divided into three parts: the sensory domain, the social dimension, and resources and methods. The thirteen authors covered a large variety of food topics ranging from the "rules" for eating Oreo cookies to the role of gender in food preparation in American households to the value of compiled cookbooks as an aid in determining dietary habits. Yet, as wide-ranging as the essays are and in spite of the editors' assertions to the contrary, few of the papers in *Foodways and Eating Habits* really demonstrate interdisciplinary scholarship. The folklorists rely almost entirely on folklore studies, the experimental psychologists depend almost exclusively on works in their own field, and so on. Unfortunately, some of these contributors also load their articles down with then-fashionable jargon in their respective fields, making their articles all but incomprehensible to readers outside the authors' area of expertise. Thus, the book is interdisciplinary primarily because the work of scholars from various disciplines appears together in the same volume.

In his 1972 article Don Yoder stressed the importance of historical and regional studies.

While much subsequent work has focused on regional foodways, folklorists have been relatively unoccupied with historical research, perhaps understandably leaving that area of investigation primarily to historians. One such effort is Peter Benes's *Foodways in the Northeast* (1984) which, despite its title that suggests an examination of contemporary northeastern foodways, is solely concerned with food-related practices in New England and New York from the late seventeenth to early nineteenth century. This book, composed of papers given at a 1982 conference on New England folklife, makes evident some of the problems with historical foodways research. When the era under scrutiny is as far back in time as that considered in Benes's volume, then one must rely totally on whatever fragments of information survive. The nine contributors to *Foodways in the Northeast* base their discussions on such varied sources as faunal remains, account books, surviving brick ovens, and court records. Thus, one has limited data over which there is little control and is confined to the aspects of foodways about which the sources have information. What's more, the contexts in which food was used are usually missing. As a result, it is very difficult to make meaningful conclusions.

There are some other problems with *Foodways in the Northeast*, the most notable being that relatively little attention is given to the social aspects of foodways. Then, too, the book is, like that of Jones, Giuliano, and Krell, interdisciplinary only in intent, for the several authors stay essentially within their own field, thereby failing to make use of potential insights gained from other disciplines. Despite its limitations, *Foodways in the Northeast* is a good example of the methodology utilized by many scholars who work exclusively in the area of historical foodways.

Another anthology that appeared in 1984 was Linda Keller Brown and Kay Mussell's *Ethnic and Regional Foodways in the United States: The Performance of Group Identity.* Like the Jones, Giuliano, and Krell volume, this one also grew out of a special issue of a journal, in this case the *Journal of American Culture,* and it shares other similarities with *Foodways and Eating Habits.*[31] The twelve contributors come from a wide assortment of disciplinary backgrounds including folklore, anthropology, nutrition, popular culture, public health, and American studies, and the book is marred by some of the same flaws found in the earlier work. There is the inevitable unevenness of a book made up of essays by several authors, especially when some of them are inclined to the overuse of jargon. Then, there is the lack of a truly interdisciplinary study despite the insistence of Brown and Mussell to the contrary. This problem is even more pronounced in *Ethnic and Regional Foodways* because much important work by social scientists, nutritionists, and folklorists is slighted or totally ignored.

*The event involving the food, rather than the food itself, is the focus. If one is to understand how food becomes a means of communication "then one of the best ways is to look at situations where its power is most heightened, in those events which also utilize the frames of play, frivolity, relaxation, or celebration."*

Not all of the shortcomings of Brown and Mussell's book are found in *Foodways and Eating Habits.* Most of the essays in *Ethnic and Regional Foodways* are reports on research in progress, which is fine. Unfortunately, Brown and Mussell, perhaps because of a longstanding academic bias that holds theory to be intrinsically superior to mere collection and research reports, present the work as though it were a theoretical tome, when in fact most of the essays do not support such a contention. Thus Brown and Mussell provide a distorted image of the book's main contribution, namely the presentation of valuable field-collected research data. *Ethnic and Regional Foodways* is also important for its discussion of issues facing foodways researchers and its proposed directions for future studies. These include analyzing the role of group allegiance and interest in shaping group identity, consideration of the role of non-ethnic or regional classifications, such as age, occupation, and socio-economic groups, in traditional foodways, the use of structuralism in studying eating as a system, and interdisciplinary interpretation.[32]

In 1988 a fourth anthology appeared, and it dealt with an aspect of foodways scholarship not covered in earlier works. While the Jones, Giuliano, and Krell volume is most concerned with the ramifications of food events, that of Brown and Mussell is primarily devoted to concepts of group and community as reflected by food traditions. In *"We Gather Together":  Food and Festival in American Life,* Theodore C. Humphrey and Lin T. Humphrey present fourteen essays that explore "the relationship between community and food at the level of the event, specifically the small group festive gathering." Here, as in the earlier works, the event involving the food, rather than the food itself, is the focus. Indeed, the editors assert that if one is to understand how food becomes a means of communication "then one of the best ways is to look at situations where its power is most heightened, in those events which also utilize the frames of play, frivolity, relaxation, or celebration."[33]

*"We Gather Together"* is much more broad-reaching than earlier works, moving as it does from small, intimate, family-centered gatherings such as birthday parties to larger community gatherings such as neighborhood booyas and city festivals. In another sense, though, the Humphreys are less ambitious than some earlier foodways scholars. The tripartite arrangement of articles—family and friends, ritual and renewal; regional specialties, work and play; and "boosterism," food and festive performance—are more accurate descriptions of the book's contents than the headings that burden *Ethnic and Regional Foodways* and suggest a theoretical stance that, for the most part, is not found in the individual essays. *"We Gather Together"* is unique in that it is the only volume on American foodways in which all of the contributors come from a folklore background but, even so, it is more interdisciplinary than some other works whose cross-disciplinary nature is more highly touted. Despite an unevenness of contributions—perhaps unavoidable in an anthology—*"We Gather Together"* is the most complete volume published to date on American foodways.

Paradoxically, American foodways scholarship has a long history and at the same time is a relatively recent area of endeavor. For more than a century folklorists have studied food and food-related practices; yet the study of American foodways is still in its infancy—it is only in the last two decades that any broad-reaching research in this area has been undertaken. Why did it take so long for folklorists to turn to the study of foodways? The answer lies in part in the traditional orientation of American folklorists. When the American Folklore Society was established in 1888 the intent was to collect and study "the fast-vanishing remains of folk lore in America—namely (a) relics of old English folk lore (ballads, tales, superstitions, etc.); (b) lore of negroes in the Southern states; (c) lore of the Indian tribes in North America (myths, tales, etc.); (d) lore of French Canada, Mexico, etc."[34] Thus, to these early folklorists the subject matter of folklore was chiefly ballads, tales, and superstitions; food simply didn't belong in the discipline and was not considered a proper area of study for folklorists. This type of thinking prevailed throughout the nineteenth century and much of the twentieth.

It must be understood that until very recently there have been relatively few American folklorists and they represented a correspondingly small variety of viewpoints. Then beginning in the 1960s, the discipline began to expand so rapidly that the American Folklore Society began to meet on its own, rather than in conjunction with other societies as in the past. This growth, which should not be overstated because folklore is still a small field when compared with history or anthropology or several other disciplines, was also manifested by a number of scholars interested in a wider concept of folklore than most of their predecessors were. As a result, subjects such as material culture and foodways, which most previous scholars thought belonged to anthropology, or some other discipline, were now considered fair game for folklorists.

Another factor inhibiting the development of extensive systematic foodways studies prior to the 1970s was the absence of any widely agreed upon plan of action. Yoder's 1972 essay went a long way towards filling this need, and thus he is rightly considered the father figure of American foodways research, even though his influence has been more that of inspiration than of theorist. Many of the currently active foodways scholars have been his students,

*This genre is potentially one of the most exciting areas of folklore because it is one of the few that affects every American.* **American Foodways,** *the only book on American foodlore that is not anthropology, illustrates how the study of foodways can reveal much about the meaning of American culture.*

but their publications often vary from the type of studies Yoder envisioned. Most folklorists writing on foodways have dealt with regional studies as Yoder suggested they should do, but few have produced historical works and even fewer have focused on survivals. Surprisingly, considering the great attention given to Appalachian folklore in the past, no folklorist has undertaken a foodways study of Appalachia, the area Yoder cited as one of the best for a foodways researcher to study. Indeed, the whole idea of relict areas hasn't been followed up by foodways scholars. Yet, whatever its limitations or lack of appeal to certain researchers, Yoder's essay has been valuable if for no other reason than that it motivated a significant number of folklorists to investigate food traditions.

Predicting the course of future folklore studies on foodways is at best risky and at worst foolhardy, because such prognostications can be little more than educated guesses. One can say with certainty that there is a small but significant body of writings upon which future foodways scholars can expand. There is also little doubt that this genre is potentially one of the most exciting areas of folklore because it is one of the few that affects every American. *American Foodways,* the only book on American foodlore that is not anthropology, illustrates how the study of foodways can reveal much about the meaning of American culture. Hopefully, it will inspire further studies, for it is desirable that current research in foodways not only continue but become more intensive and extensive.

W.K. McNeil
Ozark Folk Center
Mountain View, Arkansas

## NOTES

[1] In a letter to his friend William D. O'Conner, Hearn states, "I think a man must devote himself to one thing in order to succeed: so I have pledged me to the worship of the Odd, the Queer, the Strange, the Exotic, the Monstrous. It quite suits my temperament." He adds, "Enormous and lurid facts are certainly worthy of more artistic study than they generally receive." The quote is from Elizabeth Bisland, ed., *The Life and Letters of Lafcadio Hearn* (Boston: Houghton, Mifflin and Company, 1906), vol. 1, pp. 328–29.

[2] Writing to a friend, Hearn admits he hired a foreign cook rather than exist on Japanese fare, an act for which he feels compelled to apologize. "I am very much ashamed! But the fault is neither mine nor that of the Japanese: it is the fault of my ancestors, the ferocious, wolfish hereditary instincts and tendencies of boreal mankind." Bisland, vol. 2, p. 32.

[3] See F.A. de Caro, "A History of Folklife Research in Louisiana," in Nicholas R. Spitzer, ed. *Louisiana Folklife: A Guide to the State* (Baton Rouge: Louisiana Folklife Program/Division for the Arts and Center for Gulf South History and Culture, 1985), p. 15.

[4] The essay appeared in *Journal of American Folklore* 8 (1895): 41–71 and has been reprinted in J. Frank Dobie's *Southwestern Lore* (1931) and Simon J. Bronner's *Folklife Studies from the Gilded Age: Object, Rite, and Custom in Victorian America* (1987).

[5] Bourke, p. 41.

[6] This second essay appeared in *Journal of American Folklore* 9 (1896): 81–116.

[7] Bourke, "Folk-Foods," pp. 54–55.

[8] Ibid., p. 54.

[9] Humphrey's article appeared in *Journal of American Folklore* 58: 255–58.

[10] See, for example, Alice M. Crook, "Old Time New Mexican Usages," in J. Frank Dobie, ed., *Puro Mexicano* (Dallas: Southern Methodist University Press, 1935), pp. 184–89; Roy Holt, "Frijoles," in J. Frank Dobie, Mody C. Boatright, and Harry H. Ransom, eds., *Texian Stomping Grounds* (Dallas: Southern Methodist University Press, 1941), pp. 49–58; and Brownie McNeil, "Haymarket Plaza," in Mody C. Boatright, ed., *The Sky Is My Tipi* (Dallas: Southern Methodist University Press, 1949), pp. 168–78.

[11] Ruth Dodson's article appeared in J. Frank Dobie, Mody C. Boatright, and Harry H. Ransom, eds., *In the Shadow of History* (Dallas: Southern Methodist University Press, 1939), pp. 137–41.

[12] The book, published in 1969 by The Tate Gallery, Truchas, New Mexico, is unscholarly and, apparently, intended primarily for the tourist trade.

¹³Gonzalez's essay appears in Richard Bauman and Roger D. Abrahams, eds., *"And Other Neighborly Names": Social Process and Cultural Image in Texas Folklore* (Austin: University of Texas Press, 1981), pp. 104–22. The data on which the essay is based was gathered in interviews conducted in Los Angeles, California; Austin, Texas; and Xiutepec, Morelos, Mexico.

¹⁴Roger's comments appear in the Miscellaneous Notes section of *Dialect Notes* 4 (Part 3) (1915): 239–40.

¹⁵Underwood's article appeared in the *New York Folklore Quarterly* 3 (1947): 285–97.

¹⁶The chapter was translated by Alexander Fenton and published as "Man, Food and Milieu" in *Folk Life* 8 (1970): 45–56.

¹⁷Ibid., p. 50.

¹⁸The three articles are "Sauerkraut in the Pennsylvania Folk-Culture," *Pennsylvania Folklife* 12 (Summer, 1961): 56–69; "Schnitz in the Pennsylvania Folk-Culture," *Pennsylvania Folklife* 12 (Fall, 1961): 44–53; and "Pennsylvanians Called it Mush," *Pennsylvania Folklife* 13 (Winter, 1962–1963): 27–49.

¹⁹Yoder's article appears on pp. 325–50 of Richard M. Dorson, *Folklore and Folklife: An Introduction* (Chicago: The University of Chicago Press, 1972).

²⁰Theodore C. Humphrey and Lin T. Humphrey, eds., *"We Gather Together": Food and Festival in American Life* (Ann Arbor, Michigan: UMI Research Press, 1988), p. 4.

²¹Yoder, p. 328.

²²Ibid., p. 329.

²³Ibid., p. 332.

²⁴Ibid., p. 338.

²⁵Ibid., p. 325.

²⁶Jay Allan Anderson, "The Study of Contemporary Foodways in American Folklife Research," *Keystone Folklore Quarterly* 16 (1971): 161.

²⁷The other articles in this special issue included Roger Welsch, "We Are What We Eat: Omaha Food as Symbol," pp. 165–70; Charles Joyner, "Soul Food and the Sambo Stereotype: Foodlore from the Slave Narrative Collection," pp. 171–77; and David Hufford, "Organic Food People: Nutrition, Health, and World View," pp. 179–84.

²⁸Camp's dissertation, *America Eats: Towards a Social Definition of American Foodways*, was completed in 1978. Some of his publications based on this research include "Foodways in Everyday Life," *American Quarterly* 34 (1982): 278–89; "Food in American Culture: A Bibliographic Essay," *Journal of American Culture* 2 (1979): 559–70; and "Foodways" in William Inge, ed., *The Handbook of American Popular Culture*, vol. 2 (Westport, Connecticut: Greenwood Press, 1980); pp. 141–61.

²⁹*Foodways and Eating Habits: Directions for Research* initially appeared as *Western Folklore* 40 (1981): 1–137.

³⁰Ibid., xii.

³¹Most of this issue is given over to Linda Keller Brown and Kay Mussell, eds., "Focus on American Food and Foodways," 407–570. However, this volume, volume 2 (1979) of the *Journal of American Culture,* does contain some essays about non-foodways topics.

³²Linda Keller Brown and Kay Mussell, eds., *Ethnic and Regional Foodways in the United States: The Performance of Group Identity* (Knoxville: The University of Tennessee Press, 1984), pp. 5–15.

³³Humphrey and Humphrey, pp. 10–11.

³⁴William Wells Newell, "On the Field and Work of Journal of American Folklore," *Journal of American Folklore* 1 (1888): 3.1

# 1
# AN OVERVIEW

Every writer, scholar, cook, or critic who tackles the subject of food in and as American culture begins by citing one of several available clichés about the centrality of food in human activity. We are what we eat. The need to eat is physiologically basic; the urge to eat is instinctual. Food is important. Eating is more important. Eating well is most important—desirous, nutritionally obligatory, socially mandatory. Culture itself is the product of our search for food. Most of our time on earth is spent in obtaining, preparing, and consuming food. A great deal of time is spent cleaning up afterward, of course, but these hours need not be counted to create a statistic of impressive proportions.

In the fall of 1988, a graphic cliché that galvanized public attention, overshadowing the presidential election and other newsworthy occurrences, was what talk show host Oprah Winfrey *didn't* eat, and the dramatic change a liquid diet wrought upon her figure. Columnists have already seized upon the hour-long presentation of Ms. Winfrey's slimmer self as a rich vein of inference in the advancement of "body image" as the root cause and sum effect of human endeavor. Her apparent departure from prior eating habits suggests that we may be what we do *not* eat; among those who admire or begrudgingly acknowledge Oprah Winfrey's figurative success are many who anticipate and await her return to prior ways. This constituency adheres most firmly to the philosophy expressed in the clichés listed above—that each American man, woman, and child eats what he or she was born wanting to eat, and does so until overtaken by age, illness, or death.

These people confirm the beliefs about food and culture employed by the cliché-mongers as they adhere to ethnic, regional, religious, sexual, and age-related pat-

## HOW FOOD MEANS

*We are what we eat. The need to eat is physiologically basic; the urge to eat is instinctual. Food is important. Eating is more important. Eating well is most important—desirous, nutritionally obligatory, socially mandatory. Culture itself is the product of our search for food. Most of our time on earth is spent in obtaining, preparing, and consuming food. A great deal of time is spent cleaning up afterward, of course, but these hours need not be counted to create a statistic of impressive proportions.*

*Talking about what my
grandmother ate (and didn't)
or talking about what Oprah
eats (and doesn't)
demonstrates the centrality of
discourse about food and
culture in American life. That
seeing a box of Fiddle Faddle
conjures memories of my
grandmother is just one small
example of how food means.
That I recount the story
underscores the point. This
book is about the variety of
ways in which food
communicates culture in those
settings—home, workplace,
church hall, restaurant—where
the language of food is spoken.*

**Two children in Western wear settle down by the family pickup truck to munch on pizza. (Photo by Kay Danielson)**

terns of eating, incorporating change in diet as they incorporate change in other aspects of their lives—with hesitance and resistance. These are people who learn bad things about the foods they have enjoyed all their lives, look at themselves in a mirror, and pronounce what they see the sturdier of the two realities.

My grandmother lived into her early nineties, a thin, active woman who had lost her sense of taste to bad sinuses some time before I was born. Each workday she had a piece of pie and a cup of coffee for lunch, and usually returned to work at the family store with a bag of marshmallow candy, which she would dispense to all present. She especially favored a kind of candy which consisted of a one-inch chunk of marshmallow with a colorful slab of fruit-flavored jelly at either end, the whole then coated with granular sugar. She discovered two flavored popcorn confections in the early 1970s—Fiddle Faddle and Screaming Yellow Zonkers—and entered these snacks into her candy rotation according to an internal schedule beyond our comprehension.

My grandmother's tastes in more ordinary foods followed this schedule as well. Some seasons she ate sweet potatoes; some she ate white potatoes. In advance of her eating supper at my parents' home it was considered good manners to inquire of my aunt, with whom she lived, what kind of potatoes Grandma was eating at the moment. The fact that she could actually taste neither of them made these changing preferences mysterious to me at the time, and useful in my teaching later on as an example of food choices which could not be explained by the psychochemistry of taste.

Talking about what my grandmother ate (and didn't) or talking about what Oprah eats (and doesn't) demonstrates the centrality of discourse about food and culture in

When, in Woody Allen's film **Annie Hall**, Diane Keaton orders mayonnaise on a corned beef sandwich, her delicatessen date is embarrassed for what has been revealed. That Keaton's character does not recognize this breach of culinary syntax identifies her as an outsider to the deli world, where corned-beef-on-rye-with-mustard is not a combination of acceptable variables but a single, unalterable thing.

*Who has not tried to imagine the home lives of other people in the supermarket checkout line, based on such frail clues as their Oreos and their broccoli?  (Photo by Kay Danielson)*

American life. That seeing a box of Fiddle Faddle conjures memories of my grandmother is just one small example of how food means. That I recount the story underscores the point. This book is about the variety of ways in which food communicates culture in those settings—home, workplace, church hall, restaurant—where the language of food is spoken.

It matters little that most Americans spend more of their lives sleeping than eating or cooking. Food matters culturally because it expresses, reflects, and enacts values which are both openly attested to and privately held. The element of choice in the study of food habits defines virtually all consumer behavior as cultural business. But unlike clothing, home decoration, or musical preferences, the meanings of food choices are not so easily demonstrated or codified. Even when codes of dress or decor are implied, they are commonly understood as having communicative power. A power suit means business. A brass door knocker means colonial, or traditional, values—at least aesthetic ones.

Food is too diffuse to be so easily read. The person ahead in a supermarket checkout line, buying a half-dozen eggs and a stick of butter, may be single, elderly, or poor. At this level interpretations of food-related behavior tend to be categorical, and frequently the categories are but two—correct (or acceptable) and incorrect. When, in Woody Allen's film *Annie Hall*, Diane Keaton orders mayonnaise on a corned beef sandwich, her delicatessen date is embarrassed for what has been revealed. That Keaton's character does not recognize this breach of culinary syntax identifies her as an outsider to the deli world, where corned-beef-on-rye-with-mustard is not a combination of acceptable variables but a single, unalterable thing.

*Food matters culturally because it expresses, reflects, and enacts values which are both openly attested to and privately held.*

Rules and meanings are often discovered in their breach, not so much because the system of food and culture lacks a communicative aspect, but because the matters of who we are and what, where, how, when, and why we eat have traditionally remained separate and distinct.

## FOOD INTO FOODWAYS

*Training the lens of custom on food **and** culture brings the subject of foodways into clear perspective. Custom involves continuity. To call some aspect of behavior "customary"— whether the custom is the designation of Sunday breakfast as Dad's meal to cook, or a preference for a certain brand of cake flour—suggests that it is in keeping with established norms. However, these norms need not be formal or explicit, especially for the study of foodways, which cannot be properly limited to written or spoken communications. The informal apprenticeships that link generations of culinary practice within households and communities are largely based upon observation and imitation, frequently without reference to a communicative text of any sort. Apprentices learn by performing minor or supporting roles—preparing ingredients, setting the table, cleaning up—but benefit more from their proximity to the action than from the repetitive practice of simple skills.*

The task of the foodways student, then, is to make explicit much about food that is implicit in American culture. One might argue that food is a subject undeserving of such analysis, rooted as it is in the most fundamental of all impulses—the biologically based urge to eat. The depth and determining power of that urge, however, are better probed and measured alongside the social imperatives which accompany it. To press this point a bit further, we must look not only to those special cultural moments when all can agree that food is saying something about and for us—the cutting of a multi-tiered wedding cake, the giving of Halloween candy to masked trick-or-treaters—but also to the more ordinary customs which mark daily, weekly, and seasonal cycles of food preparation and consumption.

Such customs offer the best rationale for the use of the term "foodways." Its more commonly used cousin, "folkways," was coined by William Grant Sumner in 1906 to denote those customs, practices, and ways of thinking shared by members of the same group. In the early part of this century, research in food-related behaviors was limited to the analysis of "food habits"—dietary choices as studied by nutritionists and some anthropologists. In the early 1940s, however, John Honigmann, John Bennett, and others began to broaden the scope of dietary studies to include the social customs attendant upon food choices. They called their expanded subject "foodways." Current usage of the term, especially among folklorists and many cultural anthropologists, is broader still. In this book it simply denotes the intersection of food and culture: all aspects of food which are culture-based, as well as all aspects of culture which use or refer to food.

Training the lens of custom on food *and* culture brings the subject of foodways into clear perspective, much as a stereoscope aligns different but related images. Custom involves continuity. To call some aspect of behavior "customary"—whether the custom is the designation of Sunday breakfast as Dad's meal to cook, or a preference for a certain brand of cake flour—suggests that it is in keeping with established norms. However, these norms need not be formal or explicit, especially for the study of foodways, which cannot be properly limited to written or spoken communications. The informal apprenticeships that link generations of culinary practice within households and communities are largely based upon observation and imitation, frequently without reference to a communicative text of any sort. Apprentices learn by performing minor or supporting roles—preparing ingredients, setting the table, cleaning up—but benefit more from their proximity to the action than from the repetitive practice of simple skills.

Custom also involves the orchestration of varied social roles within complex events. Contemporary American wedding customs, for example, include not only a number of discrete practices (such as the designation of bridesmaids, the hosting of a rehearsal dinner, and the "giving away" of the bride) but also the coordination of these and many other elements to produce a "proper" ceremonial event. Custom brings the authority of accumulated experience to bear upon the present, and measures the commitment and expertise of community members according to an implicit but widely accepted way of doing things.

The shift from food to foodways does more than widen the range of the subject; it changes the definition of the things being studied from objects (food) to behaviors. The study of foodways addresses questions about the relationship between food and culture, giving equal attention and value to material and social aspects. Cultural history and ethnography have been frequently employed in the past to answer questions about the origins, popularity, or uses of certain foods, or to link specific food habits within profiles of individual or community food patterns.

However, general studies of American foodways have been few and long in coming. One reason for the delay is that as late as the early 1960s those nutritionists and anthropologists concerned with food and culture were working very much within the applied dimensions of nutritional research set in the 1930s and early 1940s by Margaret Mead and her colleagues at the National Research Council's Committee on Food Habits, an effort aimed at specific cultural problems and dietary reforms associated with World War II. The committee ultimately succeeded in broadening the emphases of food habit research, chiefly by maintaining that the nutritional problems of the Depression and World War II eras could be solved only by understanding the sources of resistance to change.

The committee consisted of equal numbers of professional anthropologists, nutritionists, and representatives of government agencies. The motivating concern of the group was not to prepare background studies of American food habits, but to provide the means by which a national nutritional campaign might establish new dietary reforms "in the culture as folk foodways," as chairman Karl Guthe put it. In a memorandum prepared in 1943 for M.L. Wilson of the U.S. Department of Agriculture, Guthe reported that the goals of the 1943 United Nations Conference on Food and Agriculture could be achieved only if the Permanent Body of the United Nations was able to:

> establish a means of integration between its program and the folkways of the many national groups it seeks to serve. . . . Unless the scientific approach can be demonstrated to the various national groups of the world as practical in terms of their own customs, habits, procedures, and values, the very foundations upon which the entire program of the United Nations Conference on Food and Agriculture are built will inevitably crumble.[1]

The American regions where the Committee on Food Habits focused much of its work were the rural Southeast and Southwest—the two areas hardest hit by the Depression and the droughts and other natural disasters of the 1930s. These areas exhibited the most serious nutritional problems, and, in the case of the Southwest, the greatest native resistance to nutritional reform.

The pressures of a continuing national emergency imbued the efforts of the Committee on Food Habits with a sense of urgency. Groundbreaking research on the food habits and customs of rural Americans was compressed into brief background studies to be used in USDA nutritional reform campaigns. But some of the right questions were being asked—among them the place of special community events in the social fabric, and the spiritual and medicinal beliefs that inform food habits.

The string of related social and public health problems which drew anthropologists into American foodways research in 1940 can be summarized as follows: The deterioration of public health is largely caused by poor food habits; poor food habits remain entrenched due to resistance to nutritional reform and reliance upon ill-informed folk (ethnic or regional) notions of proper diet and cookery; folk notions about food are generated by ethnic folkways. Twenty years after the publication of the committee's last report, the nutritional imperatives which motivated Mead and her colleagues have continued to reinforce the central importance of food habits in the study of food and culture.

Anthropologists have often found themselves working to clear the cultural underbrush to accommodate nutritional reform—thereby demanding of the people they study a measure of respect that they do not always reciprocate. Nutritionists, on the other hand, have paid closer attention to the food habits of ordinary people, and have taken a more practical approach to changing them, often looking to substitute specific foods for less nutritious alternatives without challenging the social fabric of which such choices are a part.

In the enterprise of foodways studies, there have emerged few real heroes—people who balance a comprehension of food as a system of symbols and sustenance with an abiding curiosity about and respect for the cultures that structure its meanings. Given the fairly recent approval within anthropology for the study of foodways as a cultural system, and nutritionists' natural preoccupation with health-related concerns, only a handful of professionals from either discipline has forayed into truly interdisciplinary territory. Many social scientists who have, including Ruth Benedict, Margaret Cussler, and Mary Louise de Give, or more recently, Mary Douglas and Marvin Harris, return to tell colleagues about what they have discovered without sharing information or theory about food and culture with professionals in other fields. Folklorists are often accused of the same sort of self-address, but the growing ranks of young folklorists at work documenting, analyzing, and writing about American foodways offers real hope for the gaining of new ground.

The number and dedication of these young scholars are largely the result of the work of Don Yoder, who is generally credited not only with establishing professional respect for the study of American foodways, but also with importing European ethnological approaches which have given rise to the entire folklife studies movement. Foodways studies, like folk architectural studies and the cultural interpretation of travel and tourism, have drawn theory and methods from these approaches. Yoder's imprint on contemporary foodways studies is deep but generally invisible, since his scholarship, including a series of detailed studies of Pennsylvania German life, has served to attract and encourage new research and discovery, rather than the application of a set of pre-existent theories. Thus Yoder's students, among whom I am proud to count myself, are more likely to attribute to him an openness to new approaches and allied disciplines than a particular school of thought.

A figure less well known to social scientists but a leader in foodways studies of equal stature was Dr. Dorothy Dickins, whose pioneering research among black and white Mississippians set a standard for nutritionists, public health investigators, and home economists which has yet to be met. Dickins's work was launched from the Agriculture Experiment Station at Mississippi State University in the early 1920s, where she had returned after studying at Columbia and Chicago. "Launched" is the correct term for the trajectory of her studies, since she consistently widened the scope of her research to encompass more and more of the social, cultural, and spiritual worlds of the people she studied under the guise of home economics or nutritional reform. In fact, Dorothy Dickins's doctoral dissertation was nothing less than the blueprint for an interdisciplinary field she pretty much had to herself for a half-century—family economics.[2]

As she practiced it, family economics meant the consideration of physical well-being within the social context which defined what it meant to be well. So it was that her research and publications included not only detailed comparison of the diets of black and white tenant farmers, as gathered in weekly interviews over periods of five years or more, but also studies of the vernacular architecture of the homes they built, and attitudes toward the porches where such families spent much of their time. The nutritionist's agenda and the reformer's commitment were always in evidence, but the will and ingenuity to find new approaches to abiding problems produced a rare and exemplary hybrid.

Don Yoder and Dorothy Dickens helped to deliver foodways from food habits—to find common ground and mutual respect among nutritionists, anthropologists, folklorists, home economists, and other students of food and culture for the larger enterprise to which they dedicated themselves. This book is similarly dedicated to the delivery of foodways from the confines of the kitchen and the academy.

## FINDING THE CENTER

Sometimes the surface characteristics of the subjects we study dominate our analysis of them. For instance, the textuality of the ballad defined folksong scholarship for more than two centuries, until, almost as an afterthought, the melodies that carry these words, the life stories of the people who perform them, and the settings and occasions where they are sung became recognized as integral components of our sense of the ballad. Often the technical skills required to create in a given form of expression—bobbin lacemaking, decoy carving, or bagpipe playing—are mesmerizingly rich and complex. Our curiosity becomes focused upon the task of untangling the elements of technique (the lacemaker's spools and strands) or technology (the way the bagpipe converts air into sound) that present the most immediate challenge to our ability to understand. Unfortunately, devotion to untangling these Gordian knots may leave little time to entertain other questions and challenges.

So it is with foodways. The surface characteristics of the subject—and the way we have seen it previously encountered, analyzed, and explained—provide a path to its understanding that we never think to question. Briefly stated, the most common approach to foodways is a hierarchical one which gives credence to the "natural" order of the cookery process. That is, building upon the most basic units and working toward increased variability and complexity, foodstuffs are combined (via recipes) into foods, which are in turn combined in meals. Meals are combined to form daily and seasonal regimens, which may be characterized by geography, religion, ethnicity, or other cultural factors. Culture becomes the context in which a series of food decisions is made and subsequently interpreted.

However, since authentic foodways must equally involve food *and* culture, the only thing certain about this path is that it is wrong. When the most basic significant unit in a study is material (rather than cultural), then culture becomes "factors" which may "influence" behavior, rather than the social and psychological covalent of our biologically based need for nourishment. Put another way, when foods comprise the *initial* unit of analysis, they most often become the *sole* subject of analysis. Conventional wisdom tells us that cooking is where the cultural action is; here the heritages of family and community are brought to bear upon the task of preparing food. The measurement of what individuals actually consume is considered scientific, quantitative.

In Act I, Scene 2 of Shakespeare's *Hamlet,* the Prince of Denmark bitterly criticizes his mother's speedy remarriage after the death of his father with the words, "The funeral bak'd meats did coldly furnish forth the marriage tables." A clearer example of food's significance cut free from its seemingly obvious material moorings cannot be found. Hamlet's objection to the feasts which mark the replacement of his father in the kingdom and the family has nothing to do with the actual dishes served at either the funeral or the marriage, but with the icy unification of wake and wedding into a single ceremony of criminal ascendancy. The things being compared here are events; that foods could be common to both is at once significant and utterly insignificant.

The point is that a material, hierarchical approach to foodways cannot yield the kind of comparison Hamlet makes. The smallest unit of study that reveals both the material and the social worlds in balance is the food *event*—the occasion in which food plays a part. Building upon food events, we can examine a wide variety of questions about food and culture without requiring either to be subordinate to the other. The study of food events—their makeup and variety—will unfold in the chapters that

*Ordinary people understand and employ the symbolic and cultural dimensions of food in their everyday affairs. Food is one of the most, if not the single most, visible badges of identity, pushed to the fore by people who believe their culture to be on the wane, their daughters drifting from their heritage, their sons gone uptown. Ordinary people may not write books about how food means, but they participate in an ongoing—in fact, daily—discourse on the subject more keenly cultural than anything in print.*

*What would a festival be without food—in this case, funnel cakes, ice cream, coffee, and shake-ups? (Photo by Kay Danielson)*

follow. But it is important at the outset to identify the irreducible elements of this complex whole, and to observe the balance between nature and culture, material and social elements, instinct and civilization that define foodways.

What matters is that ***ordinary people understand and employ the symbolic and cultural dimensions of food in their everyday affairs.*** Food is one of the most, if not the single most, visible badges of identity, pushed to the fore by people who believe their culture to be on the wane, their daughters drifting from their heritage, their sons gone uptown. Ordinary people may not write books about how food means, but they participate in an ongoing—in fact, daily—discourse on the subject more keenly cultural than anything in print. Academic discourse on food and culture has until very recently pretended that there is some merit in distinguishing between what people decide to eat and the culture which informs, and is in turn informed by, these "decisions."

What follows is a survey of the places in American life where food and culture intersect—places, events, and activities that reveal how culture means food and how food means culture. The survey is dotted with brief descriptions of food events from the late 1930s, including accounts of picnics, church suppers, and barbecues drawn from the Federal Writers' Project's own survey of American customs related to food and eating. These accounts illustrate the timeless discourse of American foodways—a modest and inferential way of talking about values that diminishes neither the people who hold them dear, nor the usefulness of food in making them plain.

# FOODWAYS AND AMERICAN FOLKLIFE

Although foodways is often grouped in folklife surveys with so-called material culture, the subject bridges the worlds of expression, custom, and production, and touches each of the genres of contemporary folklife. These include narratives of all sorts, including origin tales, tall tales, legends, sayings and anecdotes, jokes, and folk names, as well as personal experience narratives which comprise an important part of family and community folklore. Similarly, there is considerable variety of folksong concerning food, as well as rhymes, sung calls and hollers, and vending cries. Folk beliefs and customs associated with food range from broad characterizations of ethnic or regional tastes to occupational traditions. Material folklife includes the vernacular architecture of cook shacks, bake ovens, and picnic groves, the making and use of handmade cooking and eating utensils, the folk costume of the decorated cooking apron, and handwritten recipes—the last of these including a special sub-genre of "mock recipes" for such things as a husband or a happy marriage.

Many origin tales explain the creation or naming of an important and often distinctive local food. The story of the creation of the popcorn ball is fairly typical:

> Although most people think that someone invented the popcorn ball, a Nebraska legend has it that it is actually the product of Nebraska weather. It invented itself, so to speak, on Bergstrom Stromberg's ranch in the early days when one Febold Feboldson owned the place.
>
> During that peculiar year known as the Year of the Striped Weather, which

**ORIGIN TALES**

came between the years of the Big Rain and the Great Heat, the weather was both hot and rainy. There was a mile stripe of scorching sunshine and then a mile stripe of rain. It so happened that on Febold's farm there were both kinds of weather. The sun shone on his cornfield until the corn began to pop, while the rain washed the syrup out of his sugar cane.

Now the cane field was on a hill and the cornfield was in a valley. The syrup flowed down the hill into the popped corn and rolled it into great balls. Bergstrom says that some of them were hundreds of feet high and looked like big tennis balls at a distance. You never see any of them now, because the grasshoppers ate them all up in one day, July 21, 1874.[1]

This tale, with its elliptically named character and mammoth popcorn balls, crosses over from the basic explanatory function of an origin tale to a local tall tale. What is particularly interesting about it is how the Nebraska climate—complete with not only rapidly changing weather but grasshoppers capable of consuming a farmer's entire crop in a single day—becomes the object of the story, rather than the popcorn ball. It should be noted that north central Nebraska is an area where much of the American popcorn supply is grown, and that during the 1940s popcorn days were popular food festivals in the region.

In Vermont an American Indian source is cited for the equally accidental discovery of an equally important local food, maple syrup:

*The exaggeration that is the hallmark of the tall tale is common to many stories about food, including family stories about relatives with prodigious appetites or the spread that was laid out for a family reunion picnic.*

While Woksis, the mighty hunter, was after game, his squaw Moqua embroidered moccasins for him and boiled moose steak in the sweet water from the maple tree. She became so engrossed in fashioning a bear on the moccasins that she forgot to watch the kettle, and the water boiled away to a thick brown syrup encrusting the meat. Moqua feared the wrath of Woksis, but it was too late to remedy her error. Woksis came back, hungry from the hunt, and after some complaining about the appearance of the meat, fell to eating it. Surprise and delight showed on his coppery face as he chewed. This new dish was a gift from the Great Spirit. Woksis boasted to his tribe that Kose-kus-beh, an emissary from the happy hunting grounds, had shown his squaw how to prepare a delicious food by boiling the juice of a maple tree.[2]

The way this tale is written, and its several improbabilities (maple "water" and the "delight" of eating meat encrusted with maple syrup, to name two), suggest that the story may have its origins in children's literature or the maple sugar industry rather than the woods of Vermont.

Another regional specialty has generated at least two different stories to explain its common name, "hush puppies"—the small cornbread cakes fried in fat that commonly accompany fried fish. The first version, written in southern black dialect, appears in a description of a Georgia fish fry:

Dat's hush puppy bread. Yes sir; hit got its name from folks that was cookin' down here on the river. While dey was cookin' one day, a little dog come up and started beggin' for somethin' t' eat; a man drop down a piece of this bread and say: "Hush puppy," and dat's de way hit was named.[3]

A second account concerns a Florida fish fry:

When fish was fried in the open by early settlers, the hounds would gather around and whine and beg for food, so the fryers would quickly toss in cakes of the unsalted, unshortened meal, let it brown in the pan with all the fish flavor, and toss them to the dogs, with the admonishment, "Hush, puppy!" Hence the name. When hush puppies are made of meal with salt, shortening, an egg or two, sliced onions, and milk, they become "wampus," and are very popular at Florida fish fries.[4]

Although the descriptions of the origin of the name "hush puppy" are similar in these two accounts, it is interesting to note that in the Georgia version the plain cornmeal cakes (which are called bread) are already part of the fish fry menu. The name is attached to a pre-existent if unnamed food. In the Florida version, however, it is stated that the cooks at the fish fries simply use some of the breading for the fish to make the hush puppies. It is implied that until this use of the corn meal to keep the dogs quiet, hush puppies had not been "people food." The comparison of hush puppies to wampus seems to suggest that the latter were considered superior to, if not more common than, hush puppies as a side dish to fried fish.

## TALL TALES

The exaggeration that is the hallmark of the tall tale is common to many stories about food, including family stories about relatives with prodigious appetites or the spread that was laid out for a family reunion picnic. Few rival the proportions of the following story told about the inaugural banquet of Oklahoma Governor Jack Walton:

Jack Walton was elected governor of Oklahoma by the largest majority ever given a candidate up to that time. His inauguration was feasted by the famous Jack Walton barbecue January 8, 1923, the largest event of its kind ever held in the world's history. It lasted for three days, during which time square dancing, fiddlers' contests, and free amusements of all kinds were had. For the barbecue, there were built three 10,000 gallon coffee pots that required the steam from six steam fire engines to keep them boiling. Three carloads of coffee were used and 300,000 tin cups were distributed in the crowd. More than a mile of trenches were dug for barbecuing the meat, which consisted of one carload of Alaskan reindeer, one trainload of cattle, chickens, rabbits, and buffalo. One carload of salt and one carload of pepper were used for seasoning. Two hundred and fifty thousand buns were used. The official checkers counted over 250,000 guests who participated.[5]

An account of Texas frontier life prior to the Civil War offers a view of wild game that is similarly exaggerated:

A special dinner in those days might boast fourteen different kinds of meat.

Game was plentiful beyond belief. A red handkerchief tied around the head would attract a herd of antelope. At night the creek bottoms were black with turkeys.[6]

An Ohio cavalryman stationed in Wyoming during the Civil War wrote home with accounts of strange foods and large appetites:

> The prairie dogs are very fine to eat, being not dogs but large squirrels, although I displeased a man by telling him the potpie he had been eating was made from a bitch and five pups.
>
> It was amusing to see Major Bridger cooking his supper. He would take a whole jackrabbit and a trout about 18 inches long and put them on two sticks and set them up before the fire and eat them both without a particle of salt and drink about a quart of strong coffee. He says that when he was young he has often eaten the whole side ribs of a buffalo.[7]

## LEGENDS

Many legends associated with food date to the settlement period, when nature was full of discovery and surprise. Brigham Young's daughter Clarissa included in her memoirs an account of the first Mormon settlement concerning the lunch whistle and a famous symbol:

> Each member of the family had his own key to the gates (of the settlement) for they were kept locked after a certain time in the evening. The main entrance to the estate was the "Eagle Gate," so named from the large wooden eagle which stood guard on the pinnacle. There was a legend in the old days that every time the eagle heard the noon whistle blow he would fly straight down State Street to the old wooden watering trough, get a drink of water, and fly back again. I sat many a time with my feet in the carriage house stream, waiting for the bird to fly, but apparently was always called to dinner at the wrong time, for I never had the pleasure of seeing him in action.[8]

In Arkansas, early travel accounts relayed claims by native Americans of wondrous game to be found in the region:

> At two o'clock in the afternoon we joined the Naouydiche party; they were occupied in smoking the meat of unicorns. This is an animal as large as a medium-sized horse; it has a reddish coat, the color and length of a nanny-goat, rather slender legs, and in the middle of the forehead one horn, without branches, about half a foot in length; the meat of it is very delicious. This discovery is in accord with what M. de Bienville had heard savages say, that in the upper reaches of the river of the Ouachitas there were some unicorns.[9]

Not all of the discoveries on the frontier were so wondrous, however. Some encounters between man and nature that are captured in legend may assume a personal aspect, as this account from Washington state attests:

> The consumption of cougar meat at these (annual firefighters') repasts was impelled more from the standpoint of reprisals than from a cultivated appetite for the animal. As the story is related, a woman by the name of Minnie (Christian (sic) name unimportant) was attacked and partially devoured by one of these deadly prowlers of the woods. The surviving relatives of the family, even

to the third and fourth generation, have vowed to relentlessly track down all future offspring and descendants of the offending cougar and give vent to their wrath by eating the prey when trapped. As cougars are not too plentiful now-a-days even in the wooded country of Cowlitz County, it is quite doubtful that the family is able to provide such an animal often enough for them to become tired of the fare. But when they do enjoy such a repast, 'tis said the family always refers to the meal as "eating Aunt Minnie."[10]

As folklorist Jan Brunvand has observed, many contemporary "urban legends" reconfigure the discoveries of the frontier within the advancing technology of kitchen gadgetry. So it is that the legends Brunvand has reported reveal the suspicions people have about modern inventions like the microwave oven (drying the poodle), heavily breaded fast food (the "Kentucky fried rat"), and mechanized, post-human food companies (the mouse in the Coke bottle).[11]

## JOKES AND ANECDOTES

Jokes and anecdotes reveal the attitudes people have toward occupational and regional groups (and the attitudes these people take toward themselves) in terms of food tastes and preferences. Some examples of this regional occupational comic lore come from the mining areas of Idaho and Colorado:

> A story in point is of two later-day Highland City prospectors who, running short of grub, drew straws to see which would journey the distance into Butte City to replenish their food box. One with a hundred dollars in his pocket set out and in a day or so was seen by his partner to be trudging back over the hill with a filled gunny sack over his shoulder. Weary, the shopper entered the cabin and dropped his purchases on the table, a twenty-five-pound sack of flour and a case of quart bottles of whiskey. His partner gazed over the purchases reflectively. He hefted the liquor and then hefted the flour. "Geez, partner," he objected, "what're you goin' to do with all thet flour?"[12]

The life of the miner has generated a rich body of humor, much of which centers upon the miner's lack of patience with the conventions of polite society and his conspicuous consumption of food and liquor if and when he strikes it rich:

> The story of the Last Chance Gulch miner who made his stake is a fine example of the lone wolf in action. He rode his pack horse up to the most deluxe restaurant in what is now the capital of Montana, and startled the tuxedoed waiters by demanding, "Bring me a hundred dollars worth of ham and eggs and a bale of hay for my horse."[13]

Some humorous stories provide a more generalized image of polite culture as the foil for insider humor:

> An eastern dude stopped for supper one night at a ranch on the Huerfano River, to seek shelter for the night. Nothing was plentiful that winter but frijoles, it being an especially hard winter. On the table for supper was a large bowl of frijoles, and a bottle of pepper sauce. The beans were offered the Easterner, who refused a helping of them with an upturned nose and commented that he never ate beans. "Very well, then," came back the host, "just help yourself to the pepper sauce."[14]

## FOLK NAMING

Naming is a source of folk humor and local color, as well a useful tool in defining cultural geography. Hans Kurath's *A Word Geography of the Eastern United States* draws some of its most useful and longstanding divisions of cultural territory by charting the use of region-specific names for similar foods, among them cornbread (variously called johnny cake, pone, corn pone, and pone bread), pancake (griddle cake, fritter, hotcake, batter cake, flannel cake), and cottage cheese (curd cheese, Dutch cheese, pot cheese, smear case, and homemade cheese).[15]

George W. Featherstonhaugh, who traveled through Arkansas in 1844 and recorded his observations in *Excursion through the Slave States,* told of the naming of eating utensils. At a meal in eastern Arkansas, a servant placed on the table five knives, called "Big Butch," "Little Butch," "Old Case," "Cob-Handle," and "Granny's Knife," and five forks named "Stump Handle," "Crooky Prongs," "Horny," "Big Pewter," and "Little Pickey."[16] Featherstonhaugh was taken aback by the shortage of "proper" eating utensils in Arkansas, but saw the logic in the naming, since no two pieces looked alike and each was appropriate to not more than one eating task. This practice of naming tableware, although difficult to document more widely, is well known at least to people familiar with the Arkansas Traveler, in which five knives are referred to by name.

In Wyoming, folk names for pioneer foods carried editorial as well as humorous connotations:

*Hans Kurath charted the use of region-specific names for similar foods, among them cornbread (variously called johnny cake, pone, corn pone, and pone bread), pancake (griddle cake, fritter, hotcake, batter cake, flannel cake), and cottage cheese (curd cheese, Dutch cheese, pot cheese, smear case, and homemade cheese).*

> One ranch woman recalls that when she first served lettuce from her garden, one of the stagedrivers sheepishly said, "Pass the fodder, please." When she served shredded biscuits for the first time instead of oatmeal there was a lot of ribbing about the "baled hay." Coffee was usually called "java" and was of the Arbuckle brand. Salt side or salt pork was "sowbelly." Carrots in the Big Horn Basin after the Mormon colonists came in were referred to as "Mormon apples." Many times "pumpkin pie" was made from carrots. Fat bacon, when cooked in long strips, was called "overland trout," a bullwhacker's term.[17]

## FOLK SONGS

Folk songs about food include not only songs that draw imagery or narrative elements from the world of the edible—a category too large to describe here in detail—but also songs that precede or accompany drinking and feasting. The Winnsboro,

South Carolina, Rummy Club's annual Possum Supper, for example, had among its customs the singing of the following verse before eating:

> Now our troubles have ended
> How happy we will be
> A thousand trees surrounding us
> And a possum in every tree
> A-winking his eyes at me
> Right down under the tree
> A thousand trees surrounding us
> And a possum in every tree.[18]

Federal Writers' Project workers collected this song from ex-slaves in southern Alabama, which appears here in the dialect notation commonly used by the project:

> Bossman wants er keg o' cawn
> Hi de do hi de do
> Been drinkin' grog since he wuz bawn—
> Hi de do hi de do
> Po-leece say, "Hit's agin de law!"
> Bossman say, "Gainst de law! Ah, Pshaw,"
> I's gont'er drink ef hit's aged er raw
> Hi de do hi de do.[19]

Other folk songs measure the differences between rival territories in musical comparisons of foodways, as does this text from Nebraska:

> Come, all young girls, pay attention to my noise
> And don't fall in love with the Kansas boys
> For if you do your portion it will be
> Ash-cake and antelope is all you'll see
>
> When they get hungry and go to make bread
> They kindle a fire as high as your head
> Rake around the ashes and in they throw
> The name they give it is "doughboy's dough."
>
> When they go courtin' they take along a chair
> The first thing they say is, "Has your daddy killed a bear"
> The second thing they say when they sit down
> Is "Madam, your ash-cake is baking brown."[20]

Other lyrics, which survive as fragments of dance songs and musical calls, contain regional flourishes drawn from the Great Plains vocabulary:

> My clothes is all ragged, my language is rough
> My bread is corn-dodgers both solid and tough
> But yet I am happy, and live at my ease
> On sorghum molasses, bacon and cheese.[21]

And:

> Wake up Jacob, day's a-breakin'
> Fryin' pan's on and hoe-cake's bakin'

*Wake up Jacob, day's a-breakin'*
*Fryin' pan's on and hoe-cake's bakin'*
*Bacon in the pan, coffee in the pot*
*Git up now an' git it while it's hot*

Bacon in the pan, coffee in the pot
Git up now an' git it while it's hot.[22]

A Michigan lumberjack's meal call, also used in square dance calls, is as follows:

Run here, men, it's bilin' hot
Sam 'n Dave's both eatin' out the pot
Old Uncle Jake says "I'll be damn,
If I can't get a foreleg I'll take a ham."[23]

When the lumber boom in Michigan subsided, the lumberjacks went west with other migrants of the 1860s and 1870s, bringing this dietary caution:

Remember beans before you start
Likewise dried beef and ham
Beware of venison, damn the stuff
It's oftener a ram.[24]

Another Michigan song is said to be associated with houseraisings, at which apparently a good deal of liquor as well as food was consumed. The practice of mixing sugar with whiskey at parties is not limited to the Midwest but is common in New England and the South as well:

Whisky by the barrel
Sugar by the pound
A great big bowl to put it in
And a spoon to stir it round.[25]

Many traditional rhymes that deal with food have passed from the world of the spoken or sung advertisement to children's jump-rope, where verses are combined and split according to rhythm as well as meaning. Three rhymes collected by FWP workers from blacks in the rural South show some of this variety.

The first, from Mississippi, is a rhyme about the sweet potato that exhibits a pattern of contrast and rhythm similar to some contemporary African-American recitations:

We eat im hot, we eat im cole
We eat im young, we eat im ole
We eat im tender, we eat im tough
Un yit ay nuver got a nuff.[26]

A second rhyme was purported to be a sung advertisement for a North Carolina chittlin supper:

Good fried chittlins, crisp and brown
Ripe hard cider to wash 'em down

Cold slaw, cold pickle, sweet 'tater pie
And hot corn pone to slap your eye.[27]

The third rhyme was collected from a young black man playing the bones for tips at a South Carolina picnic:

Ham knuckle and greasy rice
Make dat man leave his wife
Ham knuckle and greasy rice
Make dat make leave his wife.[28]

This last rhyme was accompanied by one-legged dancing and the clicking of the bones.

A verbal folk art still widely practiced in those locales where open-air markets have survived is the sung or shouted vending call, or holler. The tradition has flourished in Baltimore, where public sale of produce and seafood includes not only five neighborhood marketplaces, but also the circuits of horse-drawn wagons driven by vendors called "arabbers." Photographer Roland Freeman, who himself worked the wagons in his Baltimore boyhood, has chronicled the arabbers' life in a recent photo/text study.[29]

During the summer of 1940, vendors of deviled crabs in Baltimore were heard to sing:

Crabbee, crabbee, don' you wan'
To buy my debbel cra-a-abs
Debbel, debbel, debbel cra-a-abs.[30]

That fall, when oysters were in season, the call became "OYEEE, OYE-E-E."[31]

## VENDING CALLS

*Arabbers, as street vendors in Baltimore, Maryland, are known, might direct their vending calls to a particular customer through her window. (Photo by Roland L. Freeman)*

Contemporary hollers use the musicality of the names of the foodstuffs being sold to announce their coming, and often call particular neighborhood customers by name:

> Oh, Miss Mary
> Look out your second story window
> I got watermelon red to the rind
> I got watermelon right off the vine
> Sweet strawberry, cantaloupe
> Come on out and take a look.[32]

## FOLK BELIEFS

All too often the related fields of foodways and folk medicine have been poorly distinguished, leaving the psychologies of eating and disease isolated from each other, and from the culturally based notions of food and health that are their common ground. Folk beliefs related to food range from beliefs about summoning good fortune in the gathering of foodstuffs or about insuring success in cooking to notions of luck, health, and happiness expressed in eating behavior.

Some of the most interesting of these folk beliefs have to do with the timing of certain food events or the preparation of specific foods. In North Carolina, for example, community chittlin suppers use meat from an animal killed within three days before or after a full moon. According to cooks, if this practice is not followed the "grease'll fry out of the meat" and the chittlins and other cuts will not cook properly.[33] In the cooking of barbecue for large public events, the meat must be obtained and cooked according to schedules set by the phases of the moon, and the entire event may be called off if thunder is heard on the cooking night.[34] Furthermore, tradition holds that all the cooking must be done by men, and no women may be permitted to come within smelling distance of the meat until it is time for it to be sliced. It is believed in North Carolina and Mississippi that "women stop the meat from breathing," a process required to obtain the right balance of tenderness and flavor in the meat.[35]

In South Carolina, island fisherman reportedly follow the practice of spitting on their fishbait in order to assure a good catch and observe the rhymed teaching about the relationship between wind direction and fishing conditions:

> If the wind comes from the north
>   Fish bite like a horse
> If the wind comes from the south
>   Fish bite like a louse
> If the wind comes from the east
>   They bite the least
> If the wind comes from the west
>   They bite the best.[36]

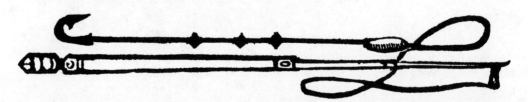

This rhyme and the belief it expresses is but one example of the rich lore of fishermen, whose success often depends upon reading an environment which offers few reliable clues to garnering a bountiful catch. Folklorists Patrick Mullen and George Carey have studied the folk beliefs of Gulf Coast and Chesapeake Bay fishermen, respectively, and their writings provide a full consideration of how folk belief functions in the waterman's world.[37]

Similar in some respects to the beliefs noted above for hogmeat and barbecue, Virginians' and South Carolinians' traditions govern the selection of turkeys and chickens for slaughter, with particular social pressure brought to bear on choices made for holiday or other large social occasions. A common practice in these states and elsewhere is the pre-selection of the fowl to be cooked, and segregation of the chosen bird for a period of two weeks or more prior to slaughtering. The diet for the bird is often different from other fowl's, and may include oat or cornmeal dough, meat scraps, or buttermilk.[38] Some cooks prefer a single-grain diet for the week before cooking in order to "clean" the bird.

*Once the turkey dinner has been eaten, the time to make a wish and break the wishbone arrives. (Photo by Kay Danielson)*

Some beliefs employ cooked food or its vestiges as "props" in the divination of luck or higher truth. A common example, of course, is the breaking of a dried chicken or turkey wishbone. These more detailed and varied divinations are gathered from the Midwest:

> If two forks, knives, or spoons are accidentally put at your place at the table, you will be married soon; if a woman cuts off thick slices of bread she will make a good step-mother; the one who takes the last piece of bread or cake on a plate will remain single; the one who takes the next-to-last piece will

marry money; if you peel an apple without allowing the peeling to break, hold it in your right hand over your head, circle it around you three times, and drop it over your left shoulder, the letter it forms will be the initial of your future husband; if you take bread when you have some, someone who is hungry is coming; you will receive mail from the direction in which your pie is pointing when it is set down at your place at the table; a piece of pie with the point toward you means a letter; with the point to one side, a package; if directly away from you, it means nothing; if you get the bubbles from your tea or coffee with your spoon before they reach the edge of the cup you will receive money.[39]

Holidays that are identified with luck or the prospect of changing fortunes abound with food-related beliefs—none more prominently than New Year's Day, as it is observed in societies following the Western calendar or other systems for marking annual time. Adherence to a yearly-repeated menu is widely believed to be useful in attracting good luck, even if the same foods the year before failed to deliver. The southern New Year's meal of hog's head and black-eyed peas has emerged as a nearly national norm as both whites and blacks from the region have carried the custom north and west with them.

Even more broadly held but less clearly stated beliefs are associated with holiday meals in general. Many households repeat the cycle of year-end holiday meals (Thanksgiving, Christmas, New Year's) in exactly the same menu and eating time, not in order to attract good fortune, but to avoid the prospect of not having successfully completed the rites of the season. It is implied, if seldom openly stated, that these are time-honored traditions, which may vary somewhat from the individual tastes of household members, but which are rooted in a system of belief and custom more fundamental than changeable food preferences.

*Many households repeat the cycle of year-end holiday meals (Thanksgiving, Christmas, New Year's) in exactly the same menu and eating time, not in order to attract good fortune, but to avoid the prospect of not having successfully completed the rites of the season. These are time-honored traditions, which may vary somewhat from the individual tastes of household members, but which are rooted in a system of belief and custom more fundamental than changeable food preferences.*

## CUSTOMS

Folk traditions governing the observation of holidays are part of the common culture which unites families and communities. Yet notions of custom and foodways range more widely over the social territory of individual habits, the identification of special family occasions, and occupational lore. The custom of eating at 6:00 p.m. (EST) on the third Sunday in January is tied to the larger and more recent custom of watching the Super Bowl. Hurry-up or prepare-ahead menus are designed for this day and published in newspapers around the country, where as great a national uniformity of behavior may be observed as on any other occasion.

Food is not the centerpiece or defining element of Superbowl Sunday, nor of Christmas, nor New Year's Day. But each of these occasions generates and maintains a number of customs particular to the larger event of which eating is an integral part. These customs, which are learned within communities as observable traditional behavior, often exhibit regional or ethnic variety, as does the account of Noche Buena written by New Mexico FWP observers in 1939:

For the most part the family is alone on Noche Buena, save for friends of the household who drop in to bring good cheer and drink a proffered cup. Above the merry din may be heard a group of youthful voices repeating some verses, the last two lines being interpreted as a harmless threat, *"Los Oremos, habran la puerta; Oremos, oremos, angelitos semos, si no nos dan"* [roughly, "Open the door, we beg you; we beg you, we beg you, we are little angels, if you don't we'll break the door down"]. By this old custom the children find many doors open to them, to add to their store of empanaditas, bizcochitos, cakes, candies, raisins, and apples given them by other householders and bulging from the bags in their hands.[40]

Such mumming customs, which are found in many cultures, traditionally feature groups of costumed revelers going from house to house requesting food treats, usually by saying or singing a standard phrase or performing a short pantomime. However, these begging visitations have changed over time. Halloween is a prime example of how tradition bends under pressures of change. No publicly practiced custom has been subjected to greater regulation, including mandated afternoon hours, the prohibition of masks, x-ray checkpoints for tampered treats, and the introduction of safer, if less tradition-based, alternative events such as neighborhood or community parties. Among the characteristics which link such modern versions of Halloween with earlier times is the mumming gift or price extracted from the householder by the stranger.

Other food customs are more explicitly connected to systems of religious belief. For example, Mormon dietary laws have spawned a variety of food customs that have become more widely characteristic of Mormon people and the communities where they are found.

Since orthodox Mormons believe in no work on Sundays, the food for Sunday dinner is prepared the night before and eaten cold the next day. This often consists of a bowl of potato salad and fried chicken or ham, put down in the cellar to keep cold. The whole family goes to church on Sunday morning and comes home at 12:30 to eat the cold dinner prepared the night before.[41]

Other dietary choices are bound to occupational turf, as revealed by the oft-quoted maxim in the West that "sheepmen eat sheep and cowmen eat cow." As recently as a half-century ago men who hired on to work for ranchers could expect their provided meals to follow this practice.[42]

Occupational foodways generally bring to mind foods that can be said to be distinctive of an occupational group, or more particularly restricted in some way by the demands of the occupation—hence the commonly held and widely popularized characterization of a cowboy's food as campfire-ready, saddlebag portable, and immune to spoilage caused by absence of refrigeration. Trail cookery books remain useful, due to the continued popularity of hiking and other outdoor recreations that simulate in a measured way the ad hoc cooking arrangements of cowboys and other saddle-bound professionals. Otherwise, few characteristics of occupational cookery are identified as distinctive from the general practices defined by region or era.

Some exceptions are worth noting—exceptions that have less to do with what people within a given occupation eat than the social or logistical circumstances in which their meals are prepared or eaten. Consider, for example, the occupational cookery of firefighters, as described by folklorist Robert McCarl and others.[43] Firefighters observe a great many of the holidays celebrated by the civilian public, with some special meals prepared in accordance with accepted general custom, along with a few—for instance, a feast to mark the promotion of a fire company member—distinctive to their trade. The foodways of firefighters, an important part of their occupational tradition, are thus defined less by the specific foods prepared than by the people preparing and eating them and the social circumstances (generally a station dining room) where meals are consumed. In company where one might assume cooking to be an undervalued skill, and where any meal might suddenly be interrupted, preparation of full-scale homecooked meals becomes a mark of pride and professional standards, as well as a note of normalcy in abnormal living conditions.

An altogether different example of occupation-based foodways was displayed on the National Mall in Washington, D.C., when Alaskan tradition-bearers were featured at the Smithsonian Institution's Festival of American Folklife. Charlene Nelson of Ketchikan, who worked as cook aboard her husband Charley's fishing boat, showed how her galley was stocked for an extended haul, and how she was able to operate within its cramped quarters. During daily cooking demonstrations at the festival, Mrs. Nelson talked about the crew's favorite foods and shared some of the quick recipes she employed to convert a small portion of the day's catch into the evening meal. What was particularly interesting and occupationally significant about her demonstrations was not the recipes, but the handwork that contributed to their preparation. For ex-

*The foodways of firefighters, an important part of their occupational tradition, are defined less by the specific foods prepared than by the people preparing and eating them and the social circumstances (generally a station dining room) where meals are consumed. In company where one might assume cooking to be an undervalued skill, and where any meal might suddenly be interrupted, preparation of full-scale homecooked meals becomes a mark of pride and professional standards, as well as a note of normalcy in abnormal living conditions.*

*Charlene Nelson, who has developed special techniques for every aspect of food preparation aboard a small boat, turns out meals for working fishermen from this galley stove. (Photo by Charles Nelson)*

*The challenge of cooking aboard the **Cheryl Ann**, a fishing boat owned by Charles Nelson of Ketchikan, Alaska, requires Nelson's wife, Charlene, to be adaptable. (Photo by Charles Nelson)*

ample, Mrs. Nelson cut up several potatoes while she described the chowder in progress on the stove. She held the potato in one hand and a small paring knife in the other, and peeled and diced the potato in a very short time without resort to a cutting board or bowl for the cut pieces. This legerdemain was a small detail, unnoticed by most of the audience, but a window on a whole range of cooking skills specially tailored to a cramped (and moving) workspace. Mrs. Nelson revealed under questioning that she had two sets of cooking techniques. Her mother had taught her one, suitable for the kitchen, and from her husband she had learned another, adapted by trial and error to the boat.

Eating customs as well as cooking customs display occupational variety. The custom of maintaining silence during meals at loggers' camps is based upon both tradition and practical considerations:

> Their silence is according to old custom: no talk at meals. Eating is a serious thing in the timber. You can't converse and do justice to the grub. Besides, the kitchen mechanics are a busy crew and like to see the loggers finish their dinner as soon as possible. It takes time to clear tables, put away food, wash pans, pots, and dishes, and get everything ready for the next morning's early breakfast. Last and most important of all, if you gab, you may not hear your neighbor's request to pass the bread, meat, or whatever, which is the height of bad manners in a logging camp dining room.[44]

## FOLK ARCHITECTURE

The folk architecture of foodways is a segment of the field that has escaped all but a few contemporary folklorists. Yet applying the criteria of *things folk* to the built or changed environment yields interesting insights into the use of space in folk culture, and the directed use of such space for food-related activities. The space allotted for the preparation and consumption of food in the American folk dwelling is difficult to define since, with the exception of permanent fixtures—plumbing, sinks, kitchen cabinets, stove, and refrigerator—all or any part of the social space in such dwellings might be used for preparing, processing, or consuming food.

In fact, any spatial description of the intersection of foodways and folk architecture should include a variety of places—gardens, yards, porches, mudrooms, kitchens, dining rooms, even parked cars. Add to the list those public or semi-public places where food events occasionally occur—school or church social halls, picnic groves, parking lots, cemeteries—and the proper emphasis begins to emerge. The folk architecture of foodways is the use of space for the production, gathering, cooking, distribution, or consumption of food, in accordance with traditionally acquired and exercised skills, values, and aesthetics, regardless of whether such space was designed to accommodate these purposes on a daily or permanent basis.

The places that are created when people set about the traditional business of foodways do have some elements in common. Their design tends to reflect the length of time they are to be occupied, the specific work which is to be done, and the social order of the people making use of them. Not all of these elements may be readily apparent; descriptions of cemetery cleaning days from North Carolina and Florida, for instance, reveal a reunion picnic masquerading as a somber work detail. Here is an account of the Florida tradition:

> The annual cemetery cleaning is a custom practiced in many small towns in north Florida. On some set date in the fall of the year, many residents drive out for an all-day picnic at the community cemetery. The purpose is to clean graves, rake paths, and plant flowers; but the event of the day is the one o'clock dinner. Food is brought by all families attending, and the best cooking of the region is offered. Chicken fried, baked, and stewed, salads of endless variety, pickles, biscuits and sweet milk, coffee and tea, watermelon and orange preserves, pies, chocolate, banana, and pineapple cakes all are spread out at once on long tables underneath the trees.
>
> To eat from one's own basket would show lack of appreciation for a neighbor's cooking. The picnickers wander along the tables selecting at will the dishes, and praising the contributions of friends. After the meal, work in the cemetery is resumed in a somewhat desultory manner.
>
> It is the procedure to clean one's own family plot, then to help with the larger plots, and finally to work on the graves of those who have no surviving relatives.[45]

There is only one phrase in this account that describes the temporary accommodations for this food event—"spread out at once on long tables under the trees." Yet it is easy to imagine how the grand display of so many dishes ("at once") and the decorum of selecting food that others had prepared might turn a graveyard into a picnic

*Participants build cribs to get ready for the Friends Meeting annual clambake in Allen's Neck, Massachusetts. (Photo by Katherine Neustadt)*

grounds, if for only an hour, and how the sharing of sampled foods and praise might reinforce the community spirit required to keep the cemetery clean. Yet consider the architecture: no cooking apparatus of any kind, no benches to sit on or tables to eat from; just a series of long tables underneath the trees.

Or consider this example: Folklorist Kathy Neustadt has written about an annual clambake in Allen's Neck, Massachusetts—a one-day event that serves over five hundred people on a spot that has no surface characteristics but a weathered concrete slab and a low stone wall near the intersection of Allen's Neck and Horseneck Roads.[46] The clambake occasions the construction of a temporary picnic grounds, a temporary ticket stand, a temporary cookhouse, and most temporary of all a log and stone structure that cooks as it burns. The appearance of this place, as it is conveyed in Neustadt's written descriptions and photographs, is the product of the cumulative history of the event—a delicate balance between the facilities necessary to serve ticket-holders and the limited human and material resources that can be summoned to accommodate these demands. The bake structure itself requires the local importation of melon-sized rocks and enough firewood to build a modest cabin for a short-statured family.

*The serious work of eating begins at the Allen's Neck clambake. (Photo by Katherine Neustadt)*

The centrality of the bake structure and the layout of the eating tables and craft displays are part of the folk architectural statement the people of Allen's Neck make each year about themselves and the guests they welcome. That the centerpiece of this temporary village is consumed by fire each year is desirable and necessary; the announcement that smoke and steam have done their work on twenty-six bushels of clams, nine hundred ears of corn, and equally serious quantities of fish, tripe, sweet potatoes, and dressing signals the commencement of the consumption that reduces the clambake to neatly gathered trash and memories.

There are other architectural extremes in American foodways, and much middle ground as well. Nails remain year after year on the west side of houses in the Southwest, where strands of chiles are hung late each summer to dry. Old refrigerators are gutted and re-outfitted by Alaskan American Indians for the smoking of native salmon. The dashboard of a (temporarily inoperative) car on the Blue Ridge is overlaid with drying pole beans. Summer kitchens, root cellars, canning cellars, spring houses, and other structures last longer than their intended functions. The living rooms in Pennsylvania where a dozen people gather to peel and core a cauldron's worth of apples, or the basement corner in western Maryland where canned goods are lined up by color—orange on the top, red in the middle, green on the bottom— these are the places where foodways and folk architecture intersect, where one day a

*There are other architectural extremes in American foodways, and much middle ground as well. Nails remain year after year on the west side of houses in the Southwest, where strands of chiles are hung late each summer to dry. Old refrigerators are gutted and re-outfitted by Alaskan American Indians for the smoking of native salmon. The dashboard of a (temporarily inoperative) car on the Blue Ridge is overlaid with drying pole beans. Summer kitchens, root cellars, canning cellars, spring houses, and other structures last longer than their intended functions. The living rooms in Pennsylvania where a dozen people gather to peel and core a cauldron's worth of apples, or the basement corner in western Maryland where canned goods are lined up on by color—orange on the top, red in the middle, green on the bottom—these are the places where foodways and folk architecture intersect, where one day a year or every night before dinner the traditions that shape a community's culture are revisited.*

year or every night before dinner the traditions that shape a community's culture are revisited.

## FOLK CRAFTS

"Craft" has two meanings in foodways—the first a narrowly defined attribute that identifies an object as having been made by hand, and the second a kind of knowing about the material world that enables an individual to make things and fix things in accordance with shared standards of beauty and function.

With an eye to the first meaning, folk craftworkers have produced much of the work which has earned them the high respect of their neighbors and more distant connoisseurs in response to demands for objects with which to gather, cook, and serve food. Baskets, pottery, knives, woven and embroidered cloth, chairs—these are objects which test the eye and hand of both the maker and the user, things which to be good must be both visually pleasing and sturdy when measured against a lifetime of use.

But folk craft is not the sum inventory of such objects. It is the generative ability to produce things in conformity with an understanding of their formal, aesthetic properties and their active place in a working world. James McCrobie, a seventh-generation white oak basketmaker from western Maryland, once showed me a basket he had made as a wedding present for his eldest daughter. It was what he called a "hot bread basket," a flattened nine-inch oval with three-inch sides. There were handles woven into the narrow ends of the oval, but even with those somewhat decorative touches the basket was small and plain, particularly in comparison with some of the larger and more complex baskets he was known for.

*Salt-and-pepper shakers come in a variety of somber or whimsical styles. (Photo by Kay Danielson)*

*The preparation and serving of food inspires many folk crafts, as shown in this stoneware, wooden bread basket, crocheted tablecloth, baskets, and wooden spoon. (Photo by Kay Danielson)*

What was special about this basket was the fact that Mr. McCrobie had mentally tucked away an expression of a particular need by his daughter. One night when she had her parents over for dinner, she had remarked that she didn't have anything in which to serve a loaf of brown'n'serve bread. Mr. McCrobie eyed the loaf and his daughter's good dishes, then spent some time thinking about how a basket to suit her needs would look and work. It needed to be deep enough to hold the bread and a cloth wrapped around it to keep it warm, but not so big as to dwarf the contents; woven closely to catch the crumbs, but smoothly so as not to snag the cloth.

For Mr. McCrobie's daughter, this was the perfect wedding present—a testimonial to her father's ability to listen as much as his ability to work with wood. He was happy to have made it exactly for her, as a blessing of sorts on the hospitality this small basket would convey to her family and guests in her new home.

In this context, it is surprising that the term "craft" is so seldom applied to the skills and generative abilities of people who work with their hands to produce, prepare, and serve food. Cooking, in particular, seems to be commonly called either a science or an art, as if the exactitude required to produce culinary perfection and the aesthetic sense to recognize it were somehow distinct from each other. Learning through extended and intimate contact the physical properties of the (edible) world, and employing that knowledge in the fashioning of appropriate—perhaps even laudable—(culinary) statements is what cookery and craft are both about.

The fact that cooks' work does not last more than a few days should not impair our appreciation of the knowledge, skill, and artistry with which the cookery process is invested. In truth, it is just as easy to find the best cake baker, sausage maker, or barbecue grillmaster in a given community as the best embroiderer or basketmaker, since communities regularly catalogue these crafts as part of their cultural assets. Even if there are no county fairs, there are ample church bake sales and community suppers to promote sound judgments about the current status of the culinary craft and its more distinguished practitioners.

So if the craft of cooking is known and recognized, why is it not counted among our cultural treasures? Because unlike the making of baskets or lace, the composition of poetry or song, cooking is not an elective art to which one may feel a calling. It is a compulsory domestic skill that is more frequently criticized in its shortcomings than praised in its successes—based upon the unforgiving premise that one who cooks is consistently and quietly good at it.

*A chef dressed for the task tries her hand at backyard barbecue. (Photo by Kay Danielson)*

*The fact that cooks' work does not last more than a few days should not impair our appreciation of the knowledge, skill, and artistry with which the cookery process is invested. In truth, it is just as easy to find the best cake baker, sausage maker, or barbecue grillmaster in a given community as the best embroiderer or basketmaker.*

## MOCK RECIPES

*"Custom" may refer to any
tradition-based practice,
including many considered so
mundane as to be subcultural.
Where food is concerned, such
customs may include the
setting of a table, the selection
of which seats are to be
occupied, and by whom, at a
dinner table, and the courtesy,
pro forma as it may be, of
requesting a copy of a recipe
at the close of a home-cooked
dinner away from home.*

In its broader usage, "custom" may refer to any tradition-based practice, including many considered so mundane as to be subcultural. Where food is concerned, such customs may include the setting of a table, the selection of which seats are to be occupied, and by whom, at a dinner table, and the courtesy, pro forma as it may be, of requesting a copy of a recipe at the close of a home-cooked dinner away from home. When instructions for something are written down and communicated in written form to others, they are technically no longer "folk." But even here the touch of tradition is evident—in the mock recipe, a subgenre of the photocopied folklore documented by folklorist Alan Dundes that has special application to foodways.[47]

These brief and usually humorous texts have dual functions—the translation of common wisdom into comically inappropriate language and format, and implied ironic commentary on the very idea of prescribing such things as the proper way to select a perfect husband, build the perfect marriage, or rear a child. Mock recipes are frequently printed in local advice columns and community newspapers, but owe much of their currency and renewed circulation to the photocopier, which, as Marshall McLuhan often said, has made every man a publisher.

The first example of this folk form is taken from a Midwestern church cookbook, and is entitled "How to Prepare a Husband":

A good many husbands are utterly spoiled in the cooking. Some women set them constantly in hot water. Others let them freeze by carelessness or indifference. Some keep them in a pickle all their lives. It is not reasonable to suppose that any husband can be tender or appetizing treated in this way, but they really are delicious when properly prepared. In selecting a husband you should not be guided by the silvery appearance, as in buying mackerel, nor by the golden tint, as in picking salmon. Be sure to select him yourself as tastes differ. Do not go to the market for him. The best are always brought to your door. But it is far better to have none unless you learn how to cook him.

(Use) a preserving kettle of the finest porcelain, but if you have nothing but an earthen pipkin it will do, with care. See that the linen in which you wrap him is nicely washed and mended with the required number of buttons or strings securely sewed on. Tie him to the kettle by a strong comfort cord. The duty cord is breakable and is apt to let him fly out of the kettle and get burnt and crusty on the edge. Set him near a clear steady fire of love, neatness, and cheerfulness. If he sputters and fizzles do not be anxious. Some do this until they are quite done. Add a little sugar in the form the confectioners call kisses, but no vinegar or pepper on any account. A little spice will improve him, but it must be used with judgement. Do not stick any sharp instruments into him to see if he is becoming tender. Stir gently, watching the while, lest he lie too flat and too close to the kettle and become flabby.

Thus treated you will find him digestible, agreeing nicely with you and the children. He will keep as long as you like, unless you become careless and set him in too cold a place.[48]

A second recipe, for "Kiss Cake," follows much the same comic logic, but in a format closer to a conventional recipe:

Take 1 armful of pretty girl, 1 lovely face, 2 laughing brown or blue eyes, 2 rosey cheeks, and 2 lips like strawberries. Mix well and press to the lips. The result will be astonishing. For frosting take 1 piece of dark piazza and a little moonlight and press into 1 large or small hand so as not to attract attention, 2 ounces of romance, and 1 or 2 whiskers. Dissolve 1–2 dozen glances into a quantity of hesitation and 2 ounces of yielding. Place kisses on blushing lips or cheeks, flavor with a slight scream, and set aside to cool.[49]

The study of folklife is the study of cultural continuity—particularly that sort of transmission which takes place beyond the bounds of such formal institutions as government, schools, and other "official" or designated arbiters of cultural practice. The two most frequently employed and widely agreed upon characteristics of things folk are informal learning of the expression or skill, and the practice of it within a community context. Using these criteria, much of American foodways is folk by definition. In fact, foodways may be the discipline that most consistently demonstrates the attributes of folklore.

The notion of informal apprenticeship, for example, is increasingly rare in the homeplace and workplace, yet remains the norm in the American kitchen. Traditionally, this apprenticeship has been described as a mother/cook/homemaker passing on domestic skills to unmarried daughters living at home. But even in families where these roles may be segmented and more varied in gender, the culture-based apprenticeship is similar, and intrinsically folk. The teaching process has an informal character; it transmits not only practical, hands-on skills but also social values that are regarded as related and inseparable elements of the same enterprise. What most cooks learn at home is a mix of information, skill, judgment, and meaning that recapitulates family, ethnic, religious, and social values.[50]

Experiences vary greatly from household to household today, but most cooking apprenticeships begin early, with children being encouraged to play with pots, pans, and utensils. As they grow older, the apportionment of mealtime tasks reveals who is being apprenticed to cook and who is relegated to non-cooking roles. Some occasions, including Christmas and other holidays for which more baking is undertaken, provide opportunities for greater responsibility, and feature custom and tradition more prominently. In this way Christmas is defined as a time for doing things at home and a time of special license for children to cook, as well as a holiday for which certain traditional foods are prepared.

Kitchen apprenticeships inculcate not only the skills necessary to prepare common foods, but also the proper way to present and serve them. How these skills translate into the young wife's first meal for her new husband is the plot for dozens of

## THE INFORMAL APPRENTICESHIP

*The informal apprenticeship, for example, is increasingly rare in the homeplace and workplace, yet remains the norm in the American kitchen. Traditionally, this apprenticeship has been described as a mother/cook/ homemaker passing on domestic skills to unmarried daughters living at home. But even in families where these roles may be segmented and more varied in gender, the culture-based apprenticeship is similar, and intrinsically folk. The teaching process has an informal character; it transmits not only practical, hands-on skills but also social values that are regarded as related and inseparable elements of the same enterprise. What most cooks learn at home is a mix of information, skill, judgment, and meaning that recapitulates family, ethnic, religious, and social values.*

situation comedy episodes and a script that is maintained in many American households with pre-set scenes, including the wife's frequent phone calls to her mother for advice and the husband's feigned appreciation of food obviously ill-prepared. In many households the event described here is preceded by a second short-term apprenticeship by the wife to her new mother-in-law, who reveals her son's tastes and preferences.

The apprenticeships that took place prior to the creation of the new household are often reenacted on special occasions such as family holiday meals, for which seniority may establish roles and apportionment of tasks irrespective of the acquired abilities of "junior" cooks. The organization of these events, and the ceremonial pecking order they create, reinforce family relationships by temporarily folding separate and far-flung households into a single family unit whose range of roles and responsibilities is idealized for the occasion.

Stereotypical as these customs may appear, they do contain elements of tradition that are invariably transmitted within the communities of the family and ethnic group. Other customs have less to do with the schooling of cooks-to-be than with the imprint of culture on time. For example, assigning Sunday supper to a time different from that of the other six suppers of the week is a tradition sustained in many households not only as a marker of the differences between Sunday and the other days of the week, but also as a convention that carries its own weight of custom. The designation of a weekly "pizza night" or other meal rotation may be more secular, but once established—usually through an instrument no more formal than a one-time suggestion—may endure as long as there are children (and adults) who anticipate and welcome it.

Other customs display elements of drama and performance which both mark special occasions and provide opportunities for skill display. A bridal couple's cutting and serving a wedding cake, for example, involves several steps that may serve as a photo opportunity culminating in the sharing of food, first with each other and then with wedding guests, in a symbolic gesture that is obligatory, traditional, and profound. The high sentiments of this occasion are prefigured in the cutting of birthday cakes, often employing heirloom cake cutters or otherwise personalized utensils, and a similar hospitality gesture. The carving of a Thanksgiving turkey in many homes is a dramatic event, conferred upon the male head of the household and performed before a seasoned and discriminating audience.

*The traditional custom of a wedding cake, cut by the bridal couple, shows how food and celebration are inextricably linked. (Photo by Erol Thibodeaux)*

Elements of verbal art, skill display, belief, folk architecture, and custom are essential ingredients of all food events, from the most simple and casual meal to the most highly charged and socially significant occasion. Subsequent sections of this book will consider how the individual chemistry of food events determines their degree of traditionality.

# 3

# THE

# FOOD EVENT

Food plays a starring or supporting role in a whole host of occasions—fish fries, church suppers, wedding receptions, Thanksgiving dinners, box socials, back yard barbecues, mother-daughter breakfasts, oyster roasts, crab derbies, burgoo feasts, and housewarmings. There ought to be a collective name for these occasions as richly suggestive as their individual labels. Until such a term presents itself, we are likely stuck with the bland phrase I have coined for these individual, and individualistic, occurrences—the "food event."

But if we are to distinguish "food events" from other kinds of events, how do we judge the centrality of food to a given event? For instance, hot dogs and popcorn are sold and eaten at a baseball game, but are they central to it? Some might argue that the term ought to refer to only those events that are primarily "about" food, i.e., those occasions for which eating serves as the recognized and ostensible pretext for the event taking place. To be sure, there are many such events, some of which are named in the previous paragraph, but it would be difficult to get too specific about measuring the degree of "foodness" an event might display, or to find consensus among its participants. It is tidier to divide all events into two categories, those in which food plays some role and those in which it does not—even if the first of these categories appears to be swelled beyond description or summary. Keep in mind that the value of considering the food event in American culture is not that such events tell us a great deal about events in general, but that by examining the intricate, varied, and often surprising ways in which food presents itself as part of our social proceedings, we can appreciate the full symbolic range and power of food in American life.

Food events, of course, are discrete and irreproducible occasions. Some kinds of events—a family reunion, for example—may place a very high value on self-replication, naturally reaching for an annual repetition of menu, participants, activities, or other factors which designate the event as an instrument of cultural continuity, a marker of time passed but more important things unchanged. A more precise example might be a couple's annual reenactment of their proposal dinner, or some other significant courtship event, for which the couple returns to a restaurant each year, often for the same meal, and in some cases to be served by the same waiter. However close these copies may come to the original, it is plain to all concerned that no two of these events are really identical, and that the attention given to replicating a given event is in some measure a rhetorical tribute to the meaning of the antecedent. The spirit of mission or progress which inspires many events—"Let's all work hard to make this year's church supper the biggest and best one yet"—may summon a specific basis of comparison (proceeds, people served) as well as a sense of history. This history is built upon individual events which may be regarded as if they were identical by the very people whose contributions insure their individuality. The fact that a church congregation considers an annual spaghetti dinner important enough to keep count of, as in "twenty-third annual . . .," says a great deal about how some people mark their own time and their relationship to a wider community. The spaghetti itself may or may not be important.

*Diners enjoy a community muskrat dinner in Michigan. (Photo courtesy of Smithsonian Institution, Office of Folklife Programs)*

*Food events include both everyday and special occasions, and their proper study must consider public and private life—wedding receptions and Sunday dinner as sides of the same coin. Much of what seems ordinary and culturally transparent is, in fact, the stuff that informs everyday decisions about who we are, how we differ from others, and why these differences matter.*

In looking at food events, one must remain skeptical of the idea that some cultural expressions are more "telling" than others, that certain occasions or activities say more than others about a culture and the people whose values they represent. For the same reasons that folklorists sometimes err in picking only the oldest and rarest expressive forms for study, it may seem natural to consider those occasions with a pre-ordained importance to be "better" examples of culture than more ordinary ones. But while events do inspire special efforts within a community, and may appear to provide more incisive views into the culture, they may not accurately reflect a more broadly defined social life. Often the exceptional behavior characteristic of important occasions represents a purposeful departure from honored norms, a disruption of routine that deliberately creates distance from the mundane.

In fact, food events include both everyday and special occasions, and their proper study must consider public and private life—wedding receptions and Sunday dinner as sides of the same coin. Much of what seems ordinary and culturally transparent is, in fact, the stuff that informs everyday decisions about who we are, how we differ from others, and why these differences matter.

In compiling a multidisciplinary bibliography of food and culture,[1] I discovered that each of the books and articles I reviewed could be placed in one of five categories, and that taken sequentially, these categories provided a balanced representation of the intersection of food and culture. The categories are:

1) Production/gathering of foodstuffs
2) Distribution of foodstuffs
3) Cookery
4) Distribution of foods
5) Consumption of food

Notice that the two activities most commonly identified as the sole or primary subject of foodways research (cookery and food consumption) are but two of five. Foodways scholars must broaden their focus to include the equally important matters of production and gathering, foodstuff distribution, and food distribution.

How does the presumed single driving force behind food-related behavior—our biologically based need to eat—generate such a rich variety of cultural expression, in custom as well as taste? At first it seems that the answer must be that culture provides form for the satiation of hunger as it does for other "instinctual" urges, such as the need to procreate. But the more closely we look at those times when food and culture are said to be in fullest flower—ritual occasions, anniversaries, holidays—the more it seems that neither the Sunday dinner nor an inaugural barbecue can be adequately described in terms of merely satisfying a primal need for nourishment. The staying power of many of these events cannot be traced solely to the quality or specialness of the foods (i.e., the twenty-third annual spaghetti dinner) or the importance of the occasion (say, the second Sunday in March).

What emerges from this puzzlement is what I have termed a "synaptic" model of food and culture, because it uses the notion of the synapse—the "gap" in brain structure and thought processes—as a metaphor. The central idea behind this model is that individual food events are created not as the expression of material (instinctual) needs alone, but by the convergence of social and biological impulses. These impulses—the needs for fellowship and sustenance—are both fulfilled in individual food events, thereby giving the events a doubled social intensity and importance. As is the case within the human brain, discrete expressions are created by the spark that bridges two realms.

This model offers a different perspective on two common questions—why food seems to find a place in even the most solemn of social occasions; and conversely why even the most ordinary meals respect the social imperative drawing together a family for a dinner hour, or creating a sense of loneliness or loss in its absence. The model may also help us to recognize that food events may be originally occasioned by either social or material needs—serving punch and cookies after an elementary school pageant to make the event more "special" or inviting the pastor to Sunday dinner; making an event into a meal or a meal into an event.

Food events are not, of course, the whole of food and culture, nor do they provide the only key to its comprehension. They are an intertwining of human business—the serving of food as a customary grace note, the expression of holiday hospitality; bread broken together symbolizing shared feelings. Subjugating the social purposes

*How does the presumed single driving force behind food-related behavior—our biologically based need to eat—generate such a rich variety of cultural expression, in custom as well as taste? At first it seems that the answer must be that culture provides form for the satiation of hunger as it does for other "instinctual" urges, such as the need to procreate. But the more closely we look at those times when food and culture are said to be in fullest flower—ritual occasions, anniversaries, holidays—the more it seems that neither the Sunday dinner nor an inaugural barbecue can be adequately described in terms of merely satisfying a primal need for nourishment. The staying power of many of these events cannot be traced solely to the quality or specialness of the foods or the importance of the occasion.*

of Thanksgiving dinner to the fulfillment of a biologically based need to eat makes no more sense than regarding this festive meal as an optional aspect of an important annual occasion. In fact, food events should be regarded as occasions which merge so-

# MEAL ORGANIZATION

## A
### PHYSICAL

**1.**
**FOOD**

FOODSTUFFS

FOOD

MENU
Fixed
Variable

**2.**
**COOKING PROCESS**

EQUIPMENT
Type
Ownership
(Individual)
(Group)

METHOD

ORGANIZATION
OF TASKS
Individual
Group

**3.**
**SITE**

SETTING
Indoor
Outdoor

TYPE
Residence
Meeting Place
Commercial
Establishment

## B
### SOCIAL

**1.**
**COOK(S)**

RACIAL/ETHNIC GROUP
OR OTHER ASSOCIATION

SEX
NUMBER

**2.**
**EATERS**

RACIAL/ETHNIC GROUP
OR OTHER ASSOCIATION

SEX
NUMBER

CONSUMPTION
Common
Differential

## A
### OCCASION

**1.**
**FREQUENCY**

DAILY

WEEKLY

ANNUAL

SEASONAL

OTHER

**2.**
**SIGNIFICANCE**

COMMEMORATIVE
Individual
Group

RELIGIOUS

RACIAL/ETHNIC

ECONOMIC
Agricultural
Occupational

POLITICAL

OTHER

## B
### RELATIONSHIP OF PARTICIPANTS

**1.**
**FAMILY**

NUCLEAR

EXTENDED

**2.**
**COMMON CHARACTERISTICS**

LOCALE

RACIAL/ETHNIC
GROUP

SEX

RELIGION

OCCUPATION

AGE

OTHER

cial and biological needs; whether one of these aspects is the instrument of the other is a judgment call best made in consideration of particular events.

Of food events in general, several interesting aspects emerge as the synaptic model is elaborated and a range of questions about a particular event is answered. These questions are summarized in the following descriptive outline of a food event, which lists important, if frequently overlooked, aspects of events. Its organization distinguishes between the meal and the event, largely in order to introduce variables associated with the "placement" of eating as an activity within larger (longer) events. Some events, for example, include more than one meal: Thanksgiving dinner may be served early in the afternoon, with guests staying for turkey sandwiches in the early evening. These and other examples are noted in the discussion that follows the outline.

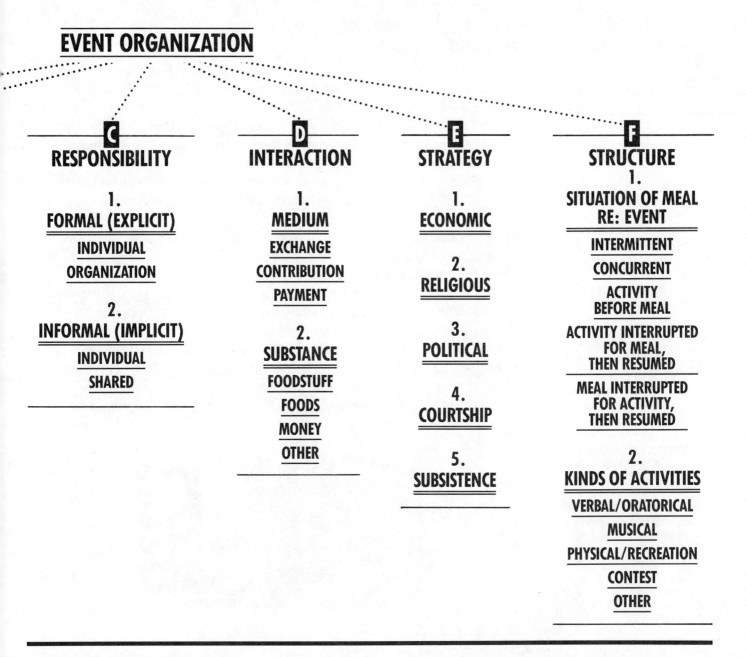

# EVENT ORGANIZATION

## C — RESPONSIBILITY

**1. FORMAL (EXPLICIT)**
INDIVIDUAL
ORGANIZATION

**2. INFORMAL (IMPLICIT)**
INDIVIDUAL
SHARED

## D — INTERACTION

**1. MEDIUM**
EXCHANGE
CONTRIBUTION
PAYMENT

**2. SUBSTANCE**
FOODSTUFF
FOODS
MONEY
OTHER

## E — STRATEGY

**1. ECONOMIC**

**2. RELIGIOUS**

**3. POLITICAL**

**4. COURTSHIP**

**5. SUBSISTENCE**

## F — STRUCTURE

**1. SITUATION OF MEAL RE: EVENT**
INTERMITTENT
CONCURRENT
ACTIVITY BEFORE MEAL
ACTIVITY INTERRUPTED FOR MEAL, THEN RESUMED
MEAL INTERRUPTED FOR ACTIVITY, THEN RESUMED

**2. KINDS OF ACTIVITIES**
VERBAL/ORATORICAL
MUSICAL
PHYSICAL/RECREATION
CONTEST
OTHER

This outline provides points of comparison for an endless variety of food events. Differences between specific events, or kinds of events, may not be particularly significant in and of themselves, but understanding these nuances enables us to hear the phrasing and inflection that give the social language its true meaning. To illustrate the point, here are accounts of four food events from the America Eats manuscript, followed by a comparison of them according to the points identified in the outline. Keep in mind that these accounts were not written according to a prescribed format, or intended to be of comparable length, style, or tone. The fact that all four are based upon their authors' firsthand familiarity with the events described, and are contemporaneous, makes them revealing not only of their ostensible subject, but also the things about these events the authors considered worthy of note. They are presented here as they appear in the original manuscript, in alphabetical order by state.

## ALL-DAY PREACHING AND DINNER-ON-THE-GROUNDS
### ALABAMA WRITERS' PROJECT [2]

In the lower end of Talledega County, in an excellent farming section somewhat remote from large towns, is a community populated strictly by native stock descendants of Confederate soldiers who made it a home after Appomattox. The settlement is non-commercial; two churches, Baptist and Methodist, and a schoolhouse comprise the center. There is little denominational rivalry, but sincere cooperation in matters affecting religion. The only visible difference is a steadfastness in adhering to separate names for the community, with the two churches bearing old-time names, only a few yards apart. The Baptists call it "Mount Sharon"; the Methodists know it as "Rocky Mount"; while the politicians from the county seat, to avoid playing favorites among a substantial group of voters, describe it as "Cahatchee neighborhood," the name of a nearby creek.

In summer, after crops are laid by, protracted meetings are held, at different times, for both churches, usually lasting a week or more and embracing at least one Sunday. On this day, assuming that it is a Methodist protracted meeting, Sunday school is held at both churches at the usual hour in the forenoon, nine o'clock, after which the Baptist meeting-house ceases to function as a church for the remainder of the day. Instead, it serves as a storage house for numerous baskets, boxes, etc., which the women of both congregations

*"At the close of the sermon, the congregation is dismissed for dinner on the grounds, to which everyone is invited and welcome, both friend and stranger. The older women gather at a selected shady spot and spread snowy tablecloths on the grass, ends touching to form a continuous 'table.' Then from baskets, boxes, and large dishpans are drawn culinary preparations that would literally tempt an epicure, and spread with a lavish hand over every available inch of the cloth. The crowd stands back in more-or-less respectful silence, waiting for the ladies to arrange the dishes to their satisfaction, and then the small boys suffer further agonies of hunger while the minister offers thanks."*

bring when they come in, an hour later, for the preaching service. The Baptist congregation adjourns to the Methodist church. The minister and deacons sit well up front among their co-laborers of the other denomination and, for all practical purposes, it is a Methodist congregation the rest of the day, few formalities of the Protestant religion drawing denominational lines.

At the close of the sermon, the congregation is dismissed for dinner on the grounds, to which everyone is invited and welcome, both friend and stranger. The older women gather at a selected shady spot and spread snowy tablecloths on the grass, ends touching to form a continuous "table." Then from baskets, boxes, and large dishpans are drawn culinary preparations that would literally tempt an epicure, and spread with a lavish hand over every available inch of the cloth. The crowd stands back in more-or-less respectful silence, waiting for the ladies to arrange the dishes to their satisfaction, and then the small boys suffer further agonies of hunger while the minister offers thanks.

Tradition requires that fried chicken be the pièce-de-résistance, and this newly-browned dish is among the first placed on the table. For this occasion it is served dry (i.e., without gravy) to facilitate eating from the hand, and the good women vie with each other to see who can bring the largest and most tempting dish. Only the choice portions are brought to the dinner; wings and necks are strictly taboo, although a few of the plumpest wings are sometimes slipped into the chicken pie to better flavor it. This latter form of chicken is not so plentiful as the fried chicken, but it is more tender and relished by the older people, eaten from plates with knife and fork.

Ranking next in popularity is ham, usually baked or barbecued, occasionally fried and served dry also. The baked ham is placed on the table intact, on a large platter, and is covered with hard-boiled eggs cut in half. It is sliced by a lady in charge, as demanded—usually steady enough to keep one person busy slicing. The occasion is deemed fitting for food of only a substantial character, especially in meats, and woe betide that newcomer who would bring "store-bought" foods, even confectionaries or cakes.

Pickles in variety: cucumber, tomato, beet; with relishes from assemblages of these, give zest to the meats. Creamed white potatoes belong here; while sweet potatoes are usually served from the pan where they are baked, sliced with sugar and spices.

Scorning bakery productions, these accomplished housewives serve real bread, either in the form of "light bread" baked in deep pans, or as nicely-browned biscuits, three or four inches high, cooked uniformly all the way through—not a "sad" spot in one. Difficult to describe for lack of a comparison, these breads possess a taste that is wanting in even the best commercial bakery products, and excuses the eater in asking for "just one more," for the seventh time.

By the time the meats have all been sampled and tested with both biscuit and light bread, to find out which is better—usually a tie—there begins to appear from the recesses of the supplementary baskets and boxes a procession of smaller receptacles containing preserves, jellies, and sweet pickles in variety that the mind of mere man can grasp as "infinite."

Side by side with these are placed cakes, pies, and custards, just as they came from the oven in tins where cooked and served from these, except "boiled custard" (an egg custard in more liquid form than ordinary) which is served in deep cups and eaten with a teaspoon. Cakes are generally of the "pound" type, with variations in recipe peculiar to nearly every woman present—a fact that serves as an excuse for eating vast quantities of cake under pretense of "trying Mrs. B's recipe." The case-hardened diners even make a repeat test with a different kind of jelly or preserves on the cake.

The most popular kind of jelly is made from crabapples, a mystery in culinary transformation that nobody except a woman can solve, with wild plums, blackberries, and muscadines contending for second place, peaches receiving honorable mention, and cherries appearing rarely. In preserves, watermelonrind stands first, with plum and peach well received, and strawberry rare but highly praised.

All of the above are on the table *in toto;* not merely one or two items, but in such abundance that gluttony has to be guarded against in visiting from table to table, as is the custom, on insistence of hospitable women, proud of their ability in preparing delightful food and generous in demonstrating it. Everyone present is pressed to partake in full measure of both substantials and delicacies, without restraint.

The dinner is eaten very leisurely, as necessary with a meal of such variety and volume. People move about from table to table, sampling a dish here, another there, and all the time being urged to "eat something." Small boys, particularly, are in their glory, for this is one time when they are permitted to eat their fill of the most choice viands, with nobody to direct or hinder. The grownups, somewhat more sedately, are not far behind in the general effort to reduce the supply of good things; exhaustion is out of the question, and when all appetites are satisfied the food yet remaining appears almost sufficient to refill the baskets and boxes from which originally taken. The excuse for this display of hospitality is that a larger crowd than usual might be on hand, and "it would never do" for the food to run short.

In mid-afternoon, the religious services are again taken up and the visitors, through courtesy to the entertaining congregation, remain.

## A TON OF RICE AND THREE RED ROOSTERS
### FLORIDA WRITERS' PROJECT [3]

Each year on Armistice Day the small Florida town of High Springs celebrates a Peanut Festival with a free chicken pilau and a full day of ceremony. The 1941 program was at once typically American and Southern. Folk from all the surrounding country began arriving in High Springs early on the morning of Armistice Day. They came crowded into old automobiles and light pickup trucks from which towheaded children dangled their legs. In spite of the area's large Negro population, the only ones in attendance were those who assisted in the preparation of the chicken pilau.

Long before ten o'clock the main street through the town's small business district was lined with expectant people waiting for the parade to begin. Participants in the parade could be seen forming a line several blocks in the distance. Finally the line moved forward at a slow pace. The procession, extending some two blocks, slowly passed a reviewing stand and was led by an American Legionnaire and a cowboy on horseback. Behind them came the Legion color guard, and then the High Springs School band, led by a shapely, high-stepping drum majorette clad in shining boots and short white satin skirt. Vying with the drum majorette for the attention of the crowd were several flashy convertible automobiles bearing the colorfully-gowned entrants in the beauty contest to select the "Queen of the Peanut Festival." The main body of the parade consisted of giggling and self-conscious schoolchildren carrying small American flags.

The parade over, the crowd broke up and hurried to a vacant lot known as the municipal park, where it formed into a semicircle around the bandstand. Assembled on the stand were the speaker of the day, a minister, several Legionnaires, a master of ceremonies, and the beauty contestants. This phase of the program was opened by the high school band playing "The Star-Spangled Banner." The men pulled off their faded farm hats, and the entire crowd stood nervously at attention.

The minister then delivered a prayer in which he asked God's blessings on America's new efforts to establish a lasting and just world peace. Following this, three local Legion officials proceeded to read an Armistice Day commentary; each man read a few paragraphs, and then passed the text on to the next. The crowd pricked up its ears a few minutes later when the master of ceremonies introduced the speaker of the day, the Honorable Jim Cary, candidate for Congress. The speaker divided his words between customary Armistice Day observations and peanuts. He spoke highly of the role the lowly peanut has come to play in the economy of the region, and told of a recent talk he had had with the famed Negro scientist, Dr. George Washington Carver, at Tuskegee Institute, "who has discovered so many uses for peanuts and all their by-products."

The master of ceremonies then proceeded to outline the coming activities. "Y'all go right ahead and do all the dancin' and cuttin' up you want to," he urged. "If ya end up in jail we can't promise to get ya out, but we'll be glad to crawl in with ya. Now after we leave here you're all invited over to the peanut oil mill. They've got a real show arranged for ya over there. 'Pee Wee' Jenkins and his Border Riders is gonna treat ya to some mighty pretty music. After that we want you all to come back over here for a big pilau dinner with all the trimmins. There's been some talk goin' round that that pilau ain't nothing but a ton of rice and three old red roosters, but I'm here to tell you that there's gonna be plenty of good chicken in that pilau and I know you're gonna like it.

"After we all git through eatin' we want to gather around the bandstand here and pick out the prettiest girl to be the Queen of the Peanut Festival, and what with all the pretty girls in the contest that looks like a mighty pleasant job. Then this afternoon comes the big game between the Alachua Indians

*"'After that we want you all to come back over here for a big pilau dinner with all the trimmins. There's been some talk goin' round that that pilau ain't nothing but a ton of rice and three old red roosters, but I'm here to tell you that there's gonna be plenty of good chicken in that pilau and I know you're gonna like it.'"*

and the High Springs Sandspurs. You folks that think there's rivalry between the university teams of Georgia and Florida haven't seen nothing yet till you've seen these here two high school teams get together. After the game tonight there's gonna be a big round- and square-dance in the high school auditorium with some more of that good music by the Border Riders. It's gonna be a fine dance, so you folks want to be sure to stay over for it. I reckon by midnight they'll all be dancin' the Elephant Stomp and by morning the band will be playing the 'Daylight Serenade.'"

Throughout the morning young girls had been handing out small bags of raw peanuts, which were not only eaten but also pinched open at the end and thus clamped on as earrings. In between the various events the men and women gathered in groups and discussed local matters, particularly the conditions of crops and the weather, and some men engaged in games of horseshoe pitching.

Preparations for the pilau had been underway since early morning, by a group of townsmen who had volunteered their services. About twenty three-legged iron kettles were assembled in the park and two Negro men kindled fires under them and got them boiling. After being dressed the chickens were boiled in the kettles and the women began the task of removing the meat from the bones. Meanwhile, huge quantities of rice were placed in the kettles and cooked in the water left over from the chicken-boilings. When the rice was done, the chicken meat was mixed with it, and stirred by a Negro man with a board. A woman with a spoon and boxes of salt and pepper went from kettle to kettle, seasoning each to taste. Nearby, a Negro man boiled coffee in a large metal drum.

Long before the pilau was ready to serve, a line of people was twisting serpentine fashion to the far reaches of the park. No one was given more than one plate, so entire families had to stand in line. The pilau was served on paper plates, accompanied by a slice of bread, a pickle, and a paper fork. Coffee was poured into paper cups and evaporated milk and sugar were provided.

The Border Riders, having been delayed by the necessity of putting away their instruments, sought to break into the line near the serving tables. But the town policeman quickly ushered them to the end of the line. "Sorry, boys," he said, "but everybody has to wait their turn."

### CONSERVATION SOCIETY DINNER
### DUBUQUE, 10/30/41
#### IOWA WRITERS' PROJECT [4]

To the music of a modern dance band, playing old-fashioned music, 500 members and guests of the Dubuque County Conservation Society partook of a fish-fry, at Melody Mill, just north of Dubuque, on the evening of October 30, 1941.

The occasion was one of fun mingled with serious business. The pavilion in which the guests were seated once stood in Union Park, a Dubuque pleasure resort popular around the turn of the century. In this old park barbecues and picnics were held and large crowds of pleasure-seekers were entertained according to the customs of those earlier years. Later, the pavilion was moved to Melody Mill, and on this gala evening in late October 1941 something of the leisure and something of the spirit of forty years ago seemed to have taken possession of the diners. Many of them were from out-of-town points—Cascade, Maquoketa, Manchester, Dyersville.

Dinner came first. It consisted of a big baked potato for each guest, cabbage salad, celery, olives, rolls, and all the walleyed pike (shipped from Lake of the Woods, Canada, and fried by chef Eddie Lyons) that anyone could eat. For dessert there was apple or pumpkin pie. Wives and daughters of Society members served this meal and during its progress the band, seated on a stage

*"'Dinner came first. It consisted of a big baked potato for each guest, cabbage salad, celery, olives, rolls, and all the walleyed pike (shipped from Lake of the Woods, Canada, and fried by chef Eddie Lyons) that anyone could eat. For dessert there was apple or pumpkin pie. Wives and daughters of Society members served this meal and during its progress the band, seated on a stage decorated with fall leaves, continued the strains of old favorites of former dances, such as "Hail, Hail, the Gang's All Here," "Shade of the Old Apple Tree," and "Stars and Stripes Forever.""'*

decorated with fall leaves, continued the strains of old favorites of former dances, such as "Hail, Hail, the Gang's All Here," "Shade of the Old Apple Tree," and "Stars and Stripes Forever."

Following the dinner came an old-fashioned community sing. Eddie Lyons, singer as well as cook, led the mixed chorus. In keeping with the spirit of the times the five hundred diners sang "God Bless America," and no one had to tell them to let themselves go and put heart into the singing.

After this came the introduction of guests. Mr. Fred T. Schwab, state conservation director and the main speaker of the evening, was introduced by Dr. W.J. Baumgartner, a director of the county association. Other introductions were by Mr. Gus Meyer, toastmaster for the evening.

The other guests consisted of Harley Lawrence, United States Wild Life Ranger; William Morf, conservation officer for Dubuque and Delaware counties; Clifford O. Johnson, instructor of biology at Dubuque Senior High School; K.M. Rooker, conservation officer for northeastern Iowa; Edward Volkert, of the Massey Wildlife Station; State Representative Robert Reilly; and George Koffman, conservation officer from Lansing. A minute of silence was observed in commemoration of the late Ross W. Harris, for many years an ardent Dubuque County conservationist.

Following the introduction of these guests came the presentation of prizes in the contest open to school children for posters and essays. County Superintendent Joseph Flynn made the presentations. The youngsters selected for awards represented the sixth, seventh, and eighth grades in Dubuque County schools, outside the city of Dubuque.

Following the presentation of prizes came the main speaker, Mr. Schwob, who outlined the danger to wildlife from the silting of streams, due in turn to soil erosion. Mr. Schwob also stressed the need for removing undesirable fish from Iowa rivers and streams, and for avoiding overstocking. Observance of these two measures insures sufficient living space to such game fish as are planted. Mr. Schwob urges that trees and other forms of cover should be restored in many parts of Iowa, and that wildlife refuges should be increased in number.

Following this and other speeches came the raffling off of prizes, which ranged from nature books and hunting knives to live turkeys and geese. For these raffle tickets were sold, and so high had enthusiasm mounted by this stage of the program that all the chances available were snatched up in a few minutes. As the successful ticket-holders claimed their prizes, many hilarious situations were revealed. Unmarried women drew men's broadcloth shirts, men found themselves the possessors of feminine gadgets that brought blushes to their cheeks and rippling laughter to the lips of the spectators. The excited cackling of two live geese and the hysterical gobbling of a live turkey mingled with this laughter and with the strains of the band to form a tapestry of earthy, homely sound.

## BOX SOCIALS
### NEBRASKA WRITERS' PROJECT [5]

Box socials have been popular in the middle-west for over half a century and still are. In Nebraska they are more common in connection with rural schools but are also to be found in the community centers of the smaller towns.

Food, if course, is the material theme of the event, but is more or less incidental to the main show and only a means to the end. The excitement, interest, and fun centers about the auctioning of the boxes, which have been prepared by the fair ladies of the district and are to be donated to a good cause, whatever it may be—extra equipment for the school room, playground, or whatnot.

This auctioning process is, in reality, a sort of lottery in which, theoretically at least, the males in attendance "buy a pig in a poke" and draw their fair supper partner, sight unseen. Actually it doesn't work out quite that way in its entirety. For some of the more popular local girls have their "steadies" and naturally will want them as supper partners for the evening. Their "steadies" are presumed to be of the same turn of mind and willing to go the limit in bidding for their favorite girl friend's box.

This circumstance leads to a little innocent skullduggery on the part of the girls, who make it a point to continue, somehow, an arrangement whereby their boyfriends will know in advance the identity of their particular boxes and bid them in. It is a little contrary to the spirit and purpose of the affair, but it does add a note of excitement, competition, and fun, not to say a little romance.

Here is how it usually works out. Let us assume that Mary is a very popular girl in the community and she has a very devoted male admirer, or even two. She proceeds to prepare a very elaborate or original box, placing the main

"Food, if course, is the material theme of the event, but is more or less incidental to the main show and only a means to the end. The excitement, interest, and fun centers about the auctioning of the boxes, which have been prepared by the fair ladies of the district and are to be donated to a good cause."

emphasis upon the decorations more likely than not. Before the box auction takes place she will see to it that her friend is informed as to the exact identity of her entry. She might, in a spirit of coquettishness or desire to stir up competition, inform not only one but an extra admirer or so. It is plain to be seen that such preliminary arrangements will not only add to the general interest and fun but to the financial results as well.

Those male admirers are going to vie with one another to bid in Mary's box and the bids should and do soar. The boys really are placed in a position where they have little choice except to lose face with the girl and possibly others.

The hour of the auction arrives and Mary's boyfriends are girded for battle. Their bidding will be limited only by the size of their pocketbooks. It is a proud Mary who will allow herself to be led off to supper by the triumphant bidder, who most likely parted company with five or ten dollars for the privilege. Her prestige in the community has risen by leaps and bounds. The successful bidder of course will be properly surprised and delighted when he opens the box and reads the name slip just as if he didn't know.

A story is told in eastern Nebraska having to do with just such a girl's mischievous grandmother, who, observing carefully the preparing of the box of her granddaughter, made up one exactly like it and managed to enter it to the confusion of all concerned. The granddaughter's big moment had been well posted in advance but of course had no advance information on Grandma's activity. The result was exactly what might have been imagined. He bid on Grandma's box for just a shade under eight dollars. The granddaughter's box, although an exact twin, sold second for less than half that amount.

The boxes which are least in demand are apt to contain the finest suppers. Coffee is furnished by the house. Such items as fried chicken, meat or cheese sandwiches, salads, biscuits, homemade bread, pickles, fruit, pie or cake, and fudge make up the bulk of the box contents.

After the supper, games or dancing or other entertainment is ordinarily available. Box socials are social entertainments with food serving only as the central theme, the prime object being to raise money for some worthy community interest or enterprise.

What should we make of these four accounts and the events described in them? In general, each represents a "type" of event situated at the intersection of food and culture. They reveal themselves in indirect ways, and by sifting through their lexicon of differences we note some interesting patterns. With reference back to the four accounts printed above, an abbreviated pass through the descriptive outline reveals culture in unexpected places.

In examining the four food events described by the Federal Writers' Project workers, we can start where most people do when describing food: how it looks just before it is eaten. The stories we tell about grand festivities and intimate occasions always seem to begin with a snapshot account of the food set before us, with details about

*The names for common food events—church supper, family picnic, crawfish boil, barbecue—conjure mental pictures of tables laden with food and people ready to attack.*

how the meal was prepared or what happened afterward surrounding this central moment. The names for common food events—church supper, family picnic, crawfish boil, barbecue—conjure mental pictures of tables laden with food and people ready to attack. These pictures open dialogue about social occasions by fixing time and place, food and mood.

The four events described by the Federal Writers Project observers differ considerably in the attention they pay to the meal within each event, and the focus of that attention. For the box supper the actual content of the suppers seems for social purposes to be incidental to the event, although there is some suggestion of foods commonly prepared for the boxes and the domestic skill which may be attached to these offerings. In fact, other accounts of box suppers invest the preparation of individual, named boxes with much more social importance as indicators of cooking ability—which may reflect not only upon the young woman responsible for fixing the supper, but also upon her family, which is responsible for the cultivation of domestic abilities. Although the setting is specified, the nature of the event seems not to rely upon any particular locale for its ability to generate conspiracy and courtship.

The description of the rice pilau dinner gives greatest attention to the cookery process, and is the only one of the four which identifies a common stock of cooking equipment employed in preparing the feast. The pilau also places importance on the selection of foodstuffs—the reference to having a few "old roosters" versus plenty of young chicken to flavor the rice. Of the four events, this is the only one which happens in its entirety in full public view; the cooking, serving, and eating all take place where the claims of quantity and quality can be visibly measured.

The menu for the conservation society dinner may vary from year to year, but the

*As participants arrive at a church supper in Tennessee, they stash their still-covered goodies on long serving tables. (Photo courtesy of Smithsonian Institution, Office of Folklife Programs)*

link between the goals of the organization, the evening's program, and the food served raises an interesting issue about philosophy and practice. Having eaten all the walleye pike they can manage, the dinner guests listen to a speech about conservation of game fish in Iowa streams. Perhaps the fact that the fish was brought in from Canada obviates the issue, but there is no suggestion in the description of the event that the culinary and programmatic agendas for the evening intersect. Actually, the fact that this issue seems striking at all is due to its continued currency; dinners for causes of all sorts have remained overwhelmingly popular, if not obligatory, for organizations raising money and consciousness in such areas as conservation, homelessness, and world hunger. The menu and decorum for food events which are in some thematic sense "about" food—its diminishing natural supply or the consequences of its shortage—is an exceedingly sensitive issue, and one which has a considerable bearing upon how the event is judged by participants and nonparticipants alike.

The description of the all-day meeting and dinner-on-the-grounds provides the greatest detail in enumerating and distinguishing the varieties of homemade food brought to the event. Of the four accounts, this one underscores the correspondence between food and social currency most clearly—the sampling of dishes as a gesture of courtesy and fellowship, the cumulative display of the variety, and the competition between cooks within established expectations and standards are all social purposes addressed within these proceedings. Unlike in the pilau account, however, the "how" of the cookery is utterly absent, save the implied credential of home cooking. Two details in the account underscore this point—the admonition to newcomers that store-bought cakes are frowned upon, and the comment that there is some measure of competition to produce the largest platter of fried chicken. If the true scale of measure in this competition is a social one—the degree to which the cook truly extends her hospitality (as a household "welcoming" others) and fellowship (as one of many sharing)—then a large platter of chicken is doubly appropriate.

Another interesting element of these four accounts has to do with the physical dimensions of the meals they describe, but not the consuming of foods prepared for them. In a slightly different way, each accounts points up a non-eating aspect of food that has distinct cultural content. As prelude to the chicken pilau, young girls pass out small bags of raw peanuts, some of which end up adorning the ears of participants. Live turkeys and geese are raffled at the conservation society dinner. A good amount of the food brought to the protracted meeting is displayed but not eaten. And the box suppers auctioned at the social are repeatedly referred to as the social pretext for the event rather than food.

Obviously, none of these non-consuming uses of foodstuffs or foods stands at any great distance from their potential to be consumed. Community-based food festivals routinely turn every available space, facility, and activity into a reflection of their adopted crop—in this case the peanut. Thus the role of a particular foodstuff in community life may be enlarged and made more visible. The turkeys and geese are raffle prizes, not intended to be consumed during the conservation society dinner, but it may be assumed that sooner or later they will find their way to someone's dinner table—the winning ticketholder's, most likely. Conspicuous display of food is a common antecedent for a variety of food events, including those in which all of the displayed dishes are consumed. The box suppers are presumed to be edible by the

*Community-based food festivals routinely turn every available space, facility, and activity into a reflection of their adopted crop. Thus the role of a particular foodstuff in community life may be enlarged and made more visible.*

young men bidding for them, even if courtship intervenes between the purchase and the supper.

But it is an apparent characteristic of these four events and generally true of food events as a whole that the meal is not the only place where food is found.

## COOKS AND EATERS

*In the stereotypical "Leave It to Beaver" household where Dad comes home at 5:30 and asks Mom, "What's for dinner?" the role of cook is a badge of identity and a social constant. Taking Mom out to eat on her birthday is a special occasion not so much because a given day's domestic workload is reduced ten percent, but because suspending the role of cook, even for one night a year, literally turns the tables of social organization and creates a moment of praiseful reflection on her other attributes. Or, viewed another way, the reluctance of other family members to step into her shoes, even for a day, shows the unchallenged lock she holds on her role as cook.*

In the stereotypical "Leave It to Beaver" household where Dad comes home at 5:30 and asks Mom, "What's for dinner?" the role of cook is a badge of identity and a social constant. Taking Mom out to eat on her birthday is a special occasion not so much because a given day's domestic workload is reduced ten percent, but because suspending the role of cook, even for one night a year, literally turns the tables of social organization and creates a moment of praiseful reflection on her other attributes. Or, viewed another way, the reluctance of other family members to step into her shoes, even for a day, shows the unchallenged lock she holds on her role as cook.

Within the organization of a meal individuals may assume several roles, which vary according to the nature of the event—from Sunday dinner at home, whose participants are simply one or more cooks and one or more eaters, to a restaurant banquet, which may add to these categories several levels of organizers. Whatever the circumstances, much is to be learned by looking closely at the relationship between cooks and the people they cook for. In describing an individual event, we would want to know about these people beyond simply recording their numbers. Two interesting points of comparison emerge from this part of the outline, each of which offers a reliable way of differentiating events.

The first point of comparison examines the relationship between the cooks and the eaters: Does the latter include the former? Do they share the same ethnic or racial background?

The four food events we have been tracing could not be more varied on this point. If such events may be characterized in terms of the fairly simple question of who is cooking for whom, the four accounts provide four different answers. The box supper is actually predicated on this issue, since the cook enters the event without knowing who will share her meal. The terms of the relationship between cook and eater therefore become the source of the event's uncertainty and conspiratorial potential. Some things are certain: the cook is one person, a young woman; the eaters are the cook and one young man. The relative closure of this event, eliminating all significant variables save the identity of the supper partner, sets it apart from the other three, which by comparison seem closer to some sense of social normalcy despite their atypically large scale.

The protracted meeting implies a division between cooks and eaters which is rendered by the social structure of the event rather than by any ethnic, racial, or other distinctions. This division is created by the prevailing spirit of hospitality which defines the event, and in turn creates the need for the women who prepared the food to complete the gesture by serving it household by household, chicken leg by chicken leg. There is no provision in this event for the cook/servers to enter the throng circulating among the culinary offerings. They most likely eat after their "guests" have been taken care of, thus not actually sharing the same meal.

The conservation society dinner employs a hired cook who is not identified as a member of the society, but most certainly is an active member of the community, be-

*Pies and cakes are sliced at a Tennessee church supper. (Photo courtesy of Smithsonian Institution, Office of Folklife Programs)*

ing the designated singing leader as well as chef. The rest of the kitchen crew is identified as wives and daughters of society members, which suggests that there is no overlap (save the possibility of Eddie Lyons, the chef) between the cooks and the eaters. In this case all the people taking part in the meal are members of a formal organization that has arranged for a meal to be provided to them.

The Florida pilau is both a cooperative community effort and a closely segregated production which places people who are excluded from the proceedings (in this case, African-American men) in charge of one of its most important parts. It is not clear how some women from the community are tapped to assist the designated black cooks, but there is a clear division, even in what is otherwise presented as a hometown celebration, between those who prepare the food and those who will enjoy the fruits of their labors.

What may appear to be a small detail in all of this emerges as a useful indicator for the kind of event being described: when and where does the cook eat? Knowing the identity of the cook, and associating the food prepared with the person who prepared it, are obvious tenets of most family meals; not knowing the cook, and not associating the food with its preparer, are obvious tenets of most restaurant meals. In between are social events which have evolved a complex decorum for recognizing, accommodating, and honoring the people who prepare the food. At some church suppers, particularly those in which the kitchen staff is comprised of church members who regularly volunteer their services for such events, the staff is formally brought out of the kitchen to receive the thanks of those who have already eaten. The cooks and servers may, as another matter of custom, set food aside for themselves and sit down to it after the supper is over. At a church supper I have attended in Baltimore, a table is reserved for the kitchen staff throughout an afternoon of continuous seating. Members of the volunteer crew take their supper break a few at a time, and are served by those on duty.

Compare these accommodations to the employment of a crew of black cooks for an all-white event, who would not be expected to join company with the people who are enjoying the food they have prepared. Events such as these are contrasted against thousands of accumulated home suppers, in which the cook takes on the apron and becomes an equal, if somewhat more weary, participant in the meal. As a result, the relegation of cooks at larger, more public events is a telling index of the social distance between the people cooking and the people eating—an indication, among other things, of whether a particular church supper is an event to raise money from outsiders or a periodic in-house celebration of roots and fellowship.

A second, related point of comparison that elucidates the social organization of the meal is the distinction between common and differential consumption. By this I mean that in some food events—like the chicken pilau—everyone eats the same thing. In others—feeding time on a transcontinental airplane flight, or the box supper, for instance—people eat different things, according to the rhetoric of the event, higher social status, willingness to pay, or other considerations. This distinction reinforces in cultural terms some of the other observable differences between restaurant meals, which enable individuals to eat their "own" food, and other kinds of events, where such differentiation is logistically impossible or socially offensive. Dinner-on-the-grounds, for example, carries the custom that it is bad manners for a participant to eat food from his or her own basket. To do so is to say to one's neighbors that you prefer your own food to all others', and you refuse others' hospitality. To make such social statements within an event that is *about* fellowship is heresy.

Many people interpret a common meal as an at least temporary suspension of a status system which makes myriad distinctions between people. A typical host accommodates a dinner guest who observes a special dietary regimen not by preparing one different meal, but by adjusting what everyone has to eat; this is one of the differences between a group of friends gathered around a dinner table and an airplane full of strangers. In less obvious ways, the psychology of common consumption may be manipulated to create intentional and socially appropriate distinctions within events that generally abide by its spirit. For example, a bride and groom generally eat the same food as their guests at their wedding reception. However, custom varies on the matter of whether the wedding party is served first, as a mark of honor, or last, as the couple's first formal gesture of hospitality.

*Fellowship is underway as cooks and eaters intermingle at a church supper. (Photo courtesy of Smithsonian Institution, Office of Folklife Programs)*

The second Saturday in November; payday; the feast of Saint Anthony; the last day of school; the first night of bowling league—these are occasions, some more special or frequent than others, when people might get together and find in eating a way of marking time. Dates for church social events often conform to a calendar based upon the sense that community is built upon a rhythm of shared time, and that the interval between festivals, dances, breakfasts, and other events should be long enough to permit anticipation to build, but not so long as to loosen the threads that tie a congregation or parish together. The end of the work week, and a few extra dollars in the pocket, may be cause enough to pick up something slightly indulgent on the way home. Reasons to gather range from the sacred and fixed to the whimsical and postpone-able.

In my descriptive outline, these are the temporal circumstances of the event—what makes it an "occasion," and why it takes place when it does. How big a deal a particular event is may be indicated by the frequency with which it occurs and the fixedness of its timing. These determinants in turn affect what actually happens in the meal— what kinds of foods may be prepared and the degree of formality that governs their consumption.

The occasions for the food events we have been discussing are variously identified in the four accounts, providing a representative range of frequency and fixedness. Of the four, the box supper is least well-defined. There is nothing in the account to establish how often this event takes place, or whether its occurrence is synchronized with other events in the community's social cycle. It seems unlikely that the box supper happens in a given community very often, since one might imagine the intrigue so necessary for its chemistry wearing off with too frequent repetitions. There is nothing about the event that links it to a particular time of year, or even a particular day of the week. However, before answering "doesn't matter" to the outline's questions about this occasion, consider the facts the account provides about the amount of time spent preparing for the event, and the importance of securing a community-wide turnout. Both of these facts suggest a fair amount of advance planning and notice, not only to arrange logistically for the supper, but also to heighten the anticipation and second-guessing which are vital to it.

*The second Saturday in November; payday; the feast of Saint Anthony; the last day of school; the first night of bowling league—these are occasions, some more special or frequent than others, when people might get together and find in eating a way of marking time. Dates for church social events often conform to a calendar based upon the sense that community is built upon a rhythm of shared time, and that the interval between festivals, dances, breakfasts, and other events should be long enough to permit anticipation to build, but not so long as to loosen the threads that tie a congregation or parish together. The end of the work week, and a few extra dollars in the pocket, may be cause enough to pick up something slightly indulgent on the way home. Reasons to gather range from the sacred and fixed to the whimsical and postpone-able.*

The chicken pilau represents the opposite end of the spectrum—an event with such a variety of reasons for happening that it appears, correctly, I think, to be a consolidation of several different occasions, among them a peanut festival, the observance of Armistice Day, and the annual match-up of rival high school football teams. Although this particular combination may seem unique and puzzling, in fact many community-wide festivals appear to gravitate toward a multi-activity, multi-theme event that represents the assemblage of all of the different things people like to do when they get together, probably on an infrequent—perhaps only annual—basis. This kind of anti-planning is akin to the hero sandwich of childhood, consisting of ingredients that are not required to complement each other or contribute to the greater sandwich good, but simply appear on the eater's list of favorite foods.

The master of ceremony's speech, listing the events of the day and the places where they will occur, seems intended to insure that with all of the traversing from one site to another not more than half of the townspeople actually show up any given place at any given time. And few of the events, save the patriotic readings by local American Legionnaires and the parade, seem unique to Armistice Day. In fact, the real occasion of this multi-activity event is nearly the same as the protracted meeting and the conservation society dinner—the work's-all-done time in the fall that lies between the summer's completed labors and the winter's new cycle of activity. Farther north, community festivals such as these typically occur in late October or early November, when families enjoy a final seasonal opportunity to socialize before entering the winter's relative isolation from each other. However, the popularity of similar events in parts of the country where the local economy and culture do not close for three or four months suggests that the notion of active/inactive time does not adequately account for these social events.

The multiple occasions which define the chicken pilau are the fixed date of November 11, the Armistice Day holiday which until recently (when the more generic Veterans' Day holiday was adopted) marked the end of World War I. During the years leading up to World War II and the period of that war's early European engagements, the observance of Armistice Day was visibly heightened in many American communities, offering as it did the opportunity to integrate a contemporary message of national pride and patriotism appropriate to a growing conflict within an occasion celebrating the end of one recently concluded. There were other peanut festivals in Florida in 1941, and many took place on or near the date of the one in High Springs. The parts of the event that Stetson Kennedy considered truly southern were the music-making and dancing, and the chicken pilau itself. In fact, pilau dinners had become part of the relief regimen in the coastal South during the period that followed the Great Depression of 1929, and even then were familiar to Georgians, Carolinians, and Floridians as an appropriate and common public food event.

The mood as well as the food described for the all-day preaching and dinner-on-the-grounds seems more appropriate to midsummer than late summer. The menu may resemble that for a smaller scale family picnic, but as an annual occasion, the completion of the agricultural season is also frequently a time for spiritual fellowship and stock-taking. The date for this annual event seems variable, but appears to be chosen from a fairly short list of possible dates, including as it must a Sunday, yet avoiding other religious and secular holidays.

The Dubuque County conservation society dinner took place on October 30, 1941, but is not identified as a monthly, seasonal, or annual event. Given the number of officials present and the scale of preparations, it seems unlikely that the event took place once a month, but the exact date appears to have been set by the organization's, rather than the community's, calendar. Some details in the event mark it as an occasion that carries the meanings of the season in which it takes place—the choice of wildfowl and warm clothing as raffle prizes, an annual report on the state of the area's wildlife resources at the close of the outdoor year, and the inclusion of a community sing as part of the program.

Occasions other than those observed in these four accounts help to round out the notion of timing implied by the term. Some church suppers, for example, take place on "founders' day," the anniversary of the date on which the congregation was established. This date becomes a fixed annual occasion with both commemorative and religious significance. A birthday party, on the other hand, is both annual and commemorative, but the significance of the date is limited to the host/honoree rather than a larger community. Some occasions are fixed by calendars not of celebrants' keeping: in Washington, D.C., and elsewhere, perhaps, parties are hosted by individuals and by politically-minded organizations on election night every two years, to mark the congressional and presidential ballot count with a gathering augmented with food, drink, and television sets.

What does all this sociology have to do with food? Recalling the synapse of material and social worlds this discussion began with, the particularization of the social end of things—every decision which adds to the social chemistry of the event—prompts an elaboration of the physical dimensions of the event. Given the fact that not every culinary complement to a social event strikes the right note or proves logistically manageable, the "food side" of any occasion may take a few years to establish a repeatable rhythm. But since most new occasions—a new birthday, an anniversary, a settlement's celebration of its successful establishment—are created not whole and new but from threads unwoven from familiar cultural custom and practice, even recently established events quickly weave an institutional cocoon that resists dramatic change.

The unnamed author of the dinner-on-the-grounds description observed the func-

tional sense in the dinner menu by noting the difference between the (dry) chicken offered to meeting participants and the way this food is usually served (with gravy). Not all custom is rooted in function, and anyone who has tried to navigate a crowded cocktail party appreciates the dexterity required to keep drink and clothing intact, but the kinds of social business transacted in events usually achieves a working balance with the food side of the ledger. In practice, these are not separate accounts, but aspects of an event which thoroughly integrate status order and bake-sale supremacy, sincere worship and the heartfelt praise of good chicken.

## HOSTS AND GUESTS

Think of a food event as a party for a moment, and consider the importance, in defining and describing the event, of knowing who is invited, who is in charge, and what those present have in common. These considerations assume a special character in food events, where responsibility and its delegation are revealing, if often hidden, aspects.

The greater the number of characteristics (ethnicity, locale, religion, occupation, age, sex, avocation) the participants in a food event have in common, the more implicit the cultural communication within the event. Family food events both confirm this rule and provide an obvious exception to it: families see themselves as social organizations distinct from other sorts, even in the identification of "who's family." The notion of an extended family may have a fairly precise sociological meaning, but especially for occasions a family may reserve for itself there is no judgment more difficult for an outsider to comprehend or predict than the designation of who is family and who isn't. This is not because the term is indistinct, but because the people who are making the judgment are bringing a lifetime of shared experience to bear upon it, and their common usage of the term over than span defines what (and who) it means. The term may include different people at different times, depending upon whether the rhetoric of the occasion communicates the inclusive gathering of all near and dear (as in a wedding reception, where the fear of "leaving someone out" may be stronger than the extended designation of kin) or a smaller unit as defined by blood or logistics.

The fact that none of the four food events examined in this chapter is a family event should not diminish the importance of this category, or the specialness of its internal culture. The strong presence of family as a metaphor for many food events that bring together people with ties other than kinship testifies to the power and currency of the term.

The relationship of participants at those four events varies from avocational membership (the conservation society dinner) to religion (the protracted meeting); from age (the box supper) to locale (the rice pilau). There are other commonalities in each case, of course: the members of the Dubuque County conservation society are from the same general locale, and most likely share ethnicity, religion, and perhaps even occupation to a considerable degree. The same may be true, again to a varying extent, for the other events. But it is important to note that of all the shared attributes among those gathered, only one or two are likely to matter in a given event. That is, within the variety of identities each person maintains and exercises—Iowan, Baptist, courting-age unmarried adolescent, Anglo-Saxon, farmer, society member—the events described here enact only one or two. In doing so, they heighten not only the values and customs associated with those roles, but the temporary connections between the identity specific to the occasion, the sharing or other use of food within it, and the other activities that constitute the event.

The designation of responsibility for a food event is a part of its social organization that brings some interesting points to the surface. In this connection, the person responsible for the event is the person to whom praise for a successful event may be directed, or to whom complaints may be made. Although responsibility can mean many things, where food events are concerned it does not always fall to the person who cooked the food consumed during the event. And therein lies a comparison that gets to the heart of the social and culinary business that take place at such events. The way that responsibility is accorded identifies three different kinds of events, which reveal the functions these events may fulfill, from simple nourishment, to the reinforcement of community identity, to gestures that send messages beyond the community. Whether this responsibility is formally or informally designated, i.e., whether there is an appointed committee to "manage" the church bakesale or people simply show up on an appointed Sunday morning with something to contribute, finding out who's in charge leads to the heart of a food event and allows us to measure its spirit and intentions.

Events in which those responsible for the event and those eating the meal are the same people are few, and so minimally social as to strain the notion that an event is taking place. One example is the cemetery cleaning cited in the first chapter, wherein each participating community member packs his or her own lunch and eats it at an appointed midday mealtime. Compared to events in which food is shared, the occasion that brings this community together seems to set an appropriately somber tone for the meal as well. The contemporary "brown bag" meeting or lecture series is a similarly marginal event. Someone who brings his or her own lunch to an event and is neither encouraged nor required to share it may be expected to feel nothing more in common with fellow brown-baggers after the event than before.

The solemnity, the asociality, of these events points up our expectation that food is supposed to create communities, even temporary ones, out of people who come together for a period of time long enough to include at least one meal. The second kind of food event identified by the comparison of assigned responsibility includes such events—those which create or reinforce bonds between people by linking those responsible and those participating within a common group. Among food events, those like the all-day preaching and dinner on the grounds that organize the work to be done along lines respecting the spirit of the occasion as well as the social order are most keenly attuned to a community ethic. Assignment of responsibility? Responsibility for what? Scores of families locked in a double enthusiasm of Christian fervor and culinary one-upmanship, not one of whom would subcontract a bit of the traditional obligation to a commercial bakery—the church dinner is community via food in its fullest flower.

There are a great many reasons for groups—organizations and communities—to reach beyond internal ranks for people to organize or attend their food events. The example previously cited of a church that holds semiannual suppers for its members and an annual fundraising supper for the public demonstrates how the needs for

*Scores of families locked in a double enthusiasm of Christian fervor and culinary one-upmanship, not one of whom would subcontract a bit of the traditional obligation to a commercial bakery—the church dinner is community via food in its fullest flower.*

funds and fellowship are separately understood and pursued. Other events, including the Florida chicken pilau, employ cooking specialists who are likely to be perceived as responsible for providing a satisfactory meal, even if the extent of their participation in the event is the simple provision of a contractual service. It is not clear that Eddie Lyons, who fried the fish for the conservation society meeting, was hired to do the job, but he is most certainly singled out as the individual responsible for the success of this part of the evening's activities.

Beyond these accommodations of special cooking expertise or public patronage, many events involve one person's (or one group's) cooking for another as a gesture that may carry a variety of personal or community messages. This is certainly true for the box supper, in which an unmarried woman cooks for an unmarried (if also unidentified) man as a statement of, among other things, marital preparedness. It is also true of the protracted meeting. The tenor of the description and the overarching spirit of the event largely conceal the fact that members of one religious congregation prepare a meal for members of a different congregation, as well as their own. Thus the individual acts of sharing and fellowship that take place as each household shares what it has brought are encircled by a larger act of fellowship between the two neighboring churches and congregations. The congregation hosting the event is communally responsible for the event, and must concern itself with both levels of hospitality.

## PRETEXTS AND PURPOSES

*A version of the traditional American potluck supper became a useful part of the domestic relief effort during the 1930s when it was observed that people who were too poor to feed themselves and too proud to accept public assistance were willing to attend a community supper to which they contributed a side dish. These meals, called "fun feeds" in Nebraska and other midwestern states where they were organized by USDA and state agricultural extension services, discreetly supplemented the homecooked dishes brought by participating families with fresh surplus meat or poultry courses prepared in extension kitchens.*

What people actually exchange at food events, and the currencies they use to do so, are telling details. The medium is often as important as the message; residents who contribute food for a rent party participate differently in the event than neighbors who pay a few dollars for a evening's supper and entertainment. "Chipping in" for a pizza or splitting a restaurant bill is seen by most people as a more congenial way of paying for dinner than dividing the cost according to the number of slices eaten or the price of food and pro-rated percentage of the tip. In fact, one of the lines of division between food events that are about getting fed and those that are about being social is the presence of money; often signaled by such phrases as "Your money's no good here." The statement is a revealing cliché, since it is usually invoked in circumstances where its true meaning is "Money's no good here," i.e., this is an event that is governed by rules of hospitality, in which money is not an acceptable currency.

If this seems farfetched, consider the lengths to which restaurants are willing to go to disguise the fact that what is actually taking place is a payment of money for food bills presented quietly, face-down on the table, to be whisked off for tabulation and change rather than settled on the spot, and, in fancier venues, masking the entire transaction in a leather-covered folder that appears, disappears, and appears again at the elbow of the host.

If there are negatively charged aspects of interaction, there are also positive ones. The exchange of money for a box supper, within the context of a fundraising event, distances the cash bid from the market value of the food, thereby converting one currency into another, more acceptable one. A version of the traditional American potluck supper became a useful part of the domestic relief effort during the 1930s when it was observed that people who were too poor to feed themselves and too proud to accept public assistance were willing to attend a community supper to which they contributed a side dish. These meals, called "fun feeds" in Nebraska and other midwestern states where they were organized by USDA and state agricultural extension services, discreetly supplemented the homecooked dishes brought by participating families with fresh surplus meat or poultry courses prepared in extension kitchens.[6] And the practice of providing a meal in both exchange and thanks for a day's labor is part of the social tradition which integrates harvesting, threshing, barnraising, and other shared labors into the general fabric of community life.

The reasons why an event occurs, identified in the outline as "strategy," do not always correspond to the significance of the occasion on which it takes place. Sometimes, as in the case of the Depression-era fun feeds, the organizers' purposes are deliberately concealed, in order to allow the surface decorum of the event to set the tone for the evening. We are told that the reason why the box supper is held is to raise money for a vaguely identified school or community cause, but the substance of the event indicated its true strategy is to provide an occasion and vehicle for the expression of courting behavior.

*Consider the lengths to which restaurants are willing to go to disguise the fact that what is actually taking place is a payment of money for food bills presented quietly, face-down on the table, to be whisked off for tabulation and change rather than settled on the spot, and, in fancier venues, masking the entire transaction in a leather-covered folder that appears, disappears, and appears again at the elbow of the host.*

## TIME(S) TO EAT

How is a meal integrated with other activities within a food event? What the sequence of eating and doing other things *means* is intriguing, since different types of events hold firm to their particular social agenda as if the slightest deviation would undermine the event's appeal and effect. The chicken pilau disposes of all the speechmaking well in advance of eating time, and the conservation society always disposes of the eating part of the program well before the first speech (not counting the blessing). Organizations that sponsor food events for their membership seem almost universally to favor an eat-first-then-talk format, whether the time of the event makes it a breakfast meeting, luncheon, or dinner. The church activities that follow dinner-on-the-grounds in the description provided here seem more of a penance for the indulgence that has just occurred than the culmination of the day's activities.

In fact, the segregation of eating in one or more parts of an extended event is in itself a cultural decision that stands in contrast to custom in many communities. The idea that one should (or must) wait until mealtime to eat is a socially applied appetite-whetter and anticipation-builder that tends to be used for meals that have the most dramatic visual staging. The presentation of a turkey at the Thanksgiving table, for example, is such a major moment in many households that a secular fast is imposed for some hours ahead of mealtime. This fast is in direct opposition to the prevailing decorum for most other kinds of extended family gatherings, where it may be judged a poor hospitality performance not to have food continually available to guests from the moment they arrive until the time they leave.

The formality of an occasion like Thanksgiving can disrupt ordinary social commerce and seem artificially stringent in households where guests are accustomed to gathering in the kitchen to nibble at a meal in progress before it is served and "pick" at it afterwards as they please. In many families the Thanksgiving turkey is like a bride, fussed over by women in private, not to be seen by guests until presented in complete finery, to be given away by the senior male in the household.

The Thanksgiving meal is also accorded a special eating time in many homes, fur-

*In many families the Thanksgiving turkey is like a bride, fussed over by women in private, not to be seen by guests until presented in complete finery, to be given away by the senior male in the household.*

ther marking the specialness of the occasion and creating blocks of leisure time at hours of the day when people are unaccustomed to relaxing or socializing. In my boyhood, Thanksgiving began at my grandmother's house with a large family dinner in midafternoon, after which the men and older boys would leave to shoot pool at the Knights of Columbus Hall for an hour or two. The hall was always deserted at this

hour on the holiday, and each year it seemed strange to me to be playing at suppertime, after having eaten during prime outside playtime. At six or so the men and boys would return to the homestead, and an hour later would enjoy a second meal of turkey sandwiches, leftovers, and various desserts. Different guests, including current boyfriends or girlfriends of teenage cousins, might show up for this second meal, but were seldom included in the first. After dessert, people would begin to leave, beginning with the cousins, and ending with the departure of my grandmother's sons around eight or nine in the evening.

Why is it that the rhythms of appetites and activities that prevail all the other days of the year are suspended on the holiday? Characteristically, on such occasions that question is never discussed. Customs having to do with the time people eat, the withholding of food in advance of a special meal, and even the unusual use of free time become part of the fabric of tradition that is learned, repeated, and passed on through a lifetime. The activities deemed appropriate for food events, formal or informal, are likewise byproducts of the traditions that govern the whole of the event. Being dressed up is an often-stated reason for eliminating many everyday and favorite activities, but others that present no logistical challenge to the occasion may be ruled out simply because they "don't fit" the template of tradition. Children in particular may be befuddled by the special rules that regulate activity at family and community festivities where their parents may be hard pressed to explain why favorite toys must be left at home, or why children must find things to do that are neither physically strenuous (the risk to good clothes, again) nor too private or asocial.

Customary behavior like this may result from the measurement of each year's special food events against an idealized mental picture of such events—an image that prescribes an atmosphere rather than a more specific agenda for the day or holiday period. Other events mix eating and other activities in a less generally accepted and more idiosyncratic way, developing over time a script that may not be comprehensible to people outside the family or community, but holds with the same power of custom for those involved in the event.

This is generally true of family reunions and other large-scale, multi-activity events that take place during summer's extended daylight hours. It must be noted that in such open-ended events the presence of a meal is a virtual constant; the contribution of different dishes from different households within the family a close second in certainty. But what develops in each family as a preferred way of doing things may involve a wide variety of activities—a softball game, group sing, viewing of old home movies (the recent trend of transferring these to videocassette has made watching them a daytime event), and contests of different kinds. The relationship between meal and activity in these events is among the most complex of all food events, often including a truly intermittent pattern of several snacks or short meals intercut with games and other activities. What tends to be true, however, is that the family reunion that sets an informal tone in the organization of proceedings maintains it throughout the day's events, creating perhaps only one plenary session, midday, for a more highly orchestrated group meal and leaving the rest of the time for unscheduled pit stops.

# 4

# FROM FIELD TO TABLE

The previous chapter considered the cultural variety to be found among and within American food events. But most of the things people identify as cultural about food are not the social and material worlds within a food gathering, but sensory details that conjure these larger worlds—the recollected smell of a favorite home-cooked dish, a barbecue stand visited on family vacations, time spent working (or admiring) a household garden, a busy marketplace, a kind of candy that appeared each year before Christmas and vanished soon thereafter.

In order to describe the meaning of these details, we must consider the social as well as the culinary traditions from which they draw their conjurative power. People tend to think of certain American cities—New Orleans, Kansas City, Baltimore—as good eating cities not because of some statistical evidence comparing the number or quality of eateries to be found in these places, but because of the reputations they have earned as cities where high value is placed on good food and its enjoyment. The designation of a local specialty is a difficult thing to create and an even more difficult thing to shake—Maryland means crabs (though it used to mean chicken); Boston means lobster (or baked beans). The positive association of food and place is like the positive association of food and family, or occasion, a cultural imprint that changes the way we see and hear, taste and remember.

The five-part division of the whole of food and culture is a useful way of organizing and examining foodways and its attendant meanings. As given in the previous chapter, these divisions are (1) production and gathering of foodstuffs, (2) distribution of foodstuffs, (3) cookery, (4) distribution of foods, and (5) consumption of foods.

## PRODUCTION AND GATHERING OF FOODSTUFFS

*Which part of the universe is edible? Americans of all backgrounds who stray from familiar shelves in their local groceries may find themselves in unfamiliar territory, confronting stuff that by its presence in a food store appears to have been included in the rolls of edible things, yet fails to meet personal culture-based criteria for such membership.*

A key distinction in this organization is made between *foodstuff* and *food*—between the raw or uncooked stuff that is gathered to be cooked and the ready-to-eat food that emerges from the cooking process. The selection of foodstuffs for this preparation is contingent upon another, more fundamental inquiry—determining which part of the universe is edible. This subject attracts a great deal of popular and professional anthropological attention[1] not only because it raises an issue of fundamental human concern, but because it is answered in such a variety of conflicting ways worldwide. And as a nation which is host to continuing immigration from all parts of the globe, Americans of all backgrounds who stray from familiar shelves in their local groceries may find themselves in unfamiliar territory, confronting stuff that by its presence in a food store appears to have been included in the rolls of edible things, yet fails to meet personal culture-based criteria for such membership.

We are not talking about food preferences here, or the frequent rigidity of dietary regimen, but the implicit categories of natural and synthetic things that people believe to be potentially edible. **Potentially** is a key word here because some people can be made to believe that a sea slug or a dandelion can be prepared in a way that will permit its backdoor entry to the world of the edible, as in the often-cited wisdom, "They're good eating, but you've got to know how to cook 'em." Those who cannot or will not be so persuaded maintain with a degree of scientific certitude that certain species of things cannot be made edible by any process, and do not require a taste test to confirm their opinion.

My brother once persuaded a neighbor girl, who was eight or nine years old at the time, to try eating a spoonful of dirt because dirt, he claimed, had minerals. She agreed, and after not finding it to her liking—perhaps keyed by my brother's growing smirk—spat it out and ran to report the incident to her mother. Both my brother and the girl were punished for the incident, he for having taken advantage of the girl's naiveté and trust and she for having ignored her upbringing and common sense by putting something in her mouth that wasn't food.

This incident confirmed for both parties that there were no more discoveries to be made, for the moment at least, in the edible universe. But one of the reasons why interest—again, popular as well as professional—in similar extensions of the bounds of the edible runs so high is that judging things foodstuffs is such a deeply held cultural construction. Of all of Dorothy Dickins's writings, for example, the one piece of research which thrust her into national attention and an article in *Time* magazine was the observance of geophagy—the eating of dirt—among black Mississippians. After having pioneered studies of diet and family economics for more than fifteen years, Dickins's scholarly article on geophagy not only outshone her earlier accomplishments, it was treated by the popular press as a discovery of vestigial primitivism in rural Mississippi—a point of view which fed racist opinion at the time and posed an impediment to her ongoing studies of food and culture among black Mississippians.[2]

Geophagy is an extreme example of the exercise of culture-based judgment about what is edible and what is not. Most often geophagy is regarded as a symptom of famine-induced psychosis, but Dickins's observation of it as part of black spiritualism crossed over quickly from her initial identification of its analogy to the consumption of poison and other non-edibles in white fundamentalist churches, to her later understanding of it as a dietary characteristic of certain agrarian people. In a way that is particular to food, a direct line is drawn between "evolved" or enlightened notions of edibility and cultural, social, and even biological advancement.

How people decide what may be made edible is an inquiry which leads to the development of patterns based on individual judgments, none of which is consistent with any characteristic of the foodstuff which may be isolated. Name a characteristic of inedible things, and a group of Americans can be found who routinely defy it. There may be virtual crosscultural unanimity on some characteristics of the inedible—the color blue, for instance—but sensory characteristics tend to confirm attitudes more deeply implicit in a given culture. The conclusion is not that Americans will eat anything, but that the definition of the categories of edible and inedible is culture read as science, and that the boundaries of these categories tell us as much about cosmology as food preference.

The difference between gathering and producing foodstuffs has, of course, its own anthropological story, having to do with the evolution of the human species from hunter and gatherer to grower and producer of food. The American food industry has made all these activities—hunting for game, foraging for edible plants, gardening, and raising livestock—avocations which may dimly recall a functional purpose. Even if a zest for the sport of hunting or the fresh air swallowed during berry-picking has replaced hunger as the primary motivation for most people, the traditional appeal of these pastimes is deeply rooted. Hunting and fishing do not require the gathering of foodstuffs in quantities sufficient to feed oneself or one's family in order to justify the expenditure of time and money required to be successful, even if such productivity is used as a measure of the success of a hunting or fishing expedition.

Students of foodways have only recently begun to look at home- and community-based horticulture and husbandry as part of the culture of food. The production of ethnically special vegetables has emerged in the past decade as an issue of regulatory as well as cultural concern, since the importation of plants and seeds is strictly governed by federal law. Particularly among recent southeast Asian immigrants, the creation and cultivation of gardens that produce vegetables from native seed stock takes on a community importance akin to the preservation of more symbolic cultural traditions. The phenomena of surreptitious seed importation and basement or back yard gardens confirm both the importance of specific foods in bridging cultures and the resilience of tastes, even where apparently equivalent or similar foodstuffs may be available.

For example, Ethiopian immigrants in the Washington, D.C., area have developed an elaborate system for importing the variety of red peppers used in much of their traditional cookery which includes friends and family members bringing back large quantities of the ground spice from homelands after business or personal trips and the cultivation of small stocks of the preferred variety in window boxes and back yard plots. Of course, city markets and specialty groceries that serve the sizable Ethiopian community stock fresh and ground red peppers, as do stores serving the many other ethnic communities that use the spice. But the differences in taste and strength between the real thing and its commercially available substitute—differences too slight for most outsiders to perceive—are deemed sufficiently important for people to run the risk of having their baggage impounded and confiscated.

*A quiet moment during a day-long Cambodian wedding ceremony in Houston provides an opportunity for fellowship among honored guests. (Photo by Frank Proschan; courtesy of the American Folklife Center, Library of Congress)*

On a somewhat larger and more officially sanctioned scale, home gardening fills an increasing need for fresh foods and the confidence of knowing that what comes from the garden meets a more exacting specification than all-purpose supermarket produce. The survival of an industry of ethnic foodstores is based in part upon the proliferation of small-scale ethnic vegetable truckfarms, and in turn, the preservation of seed varieties that may no longer be commercially available. Thus gardening may be both figuratively and literally a heritage enterprise for ethnic populations.

In a larger sense, the notion of garden is deeply cultural, almost independent of what is grown or the need for growing it. The word is, after all, both a noun and a verb—a place and an activity with separate levels of function and aesthetics that often provide disguises for each other. Few people garden because they must; most who grow vegetables, fruits, and other edible foodstuffs do so for reasons they seldom voice candidly. Among the reasons why people garden are some which may be obvious to the gardener, though relatively separate from the edible outcome—the creation of a family enterprise with (educational) roles for individual members, the visible achievement of coaxing a yielding plant from a tiny seed, as a link to a real or imagined past—the parents' or grandparents' garden nostalgically remembered or an earlier America recalled.

Gardens can also produce homemade gifts for holidays and other occasions, as well as surplus crops that can be distributed in such a way as to build or reinforce community ties. But other reasons, perhaps not so apparent, and even less often cited by practitioners, may be closer to the point. Gardens provide an endless supply of things to talk about, and a better reason for talking about the weather than most non-gardeners have. Gardening offers an outlet for any excess time or income within

*Among the reasons why people garden are the creation of a family enterprise with (educational) roles for individual members, the visible achievement of coaxing a yielding plant from a tiny seed, as a link to a real or imagined past—the parents' or grandparents' garden nostalgically remembered or an earlier America recalled.*

*A gardener checks his summer vegetables at the height of their lush production. (Photo by Kay Danielson)*

the household, since the amount of work that needs to be done at the moment, or should be done to prepare for the next, is nearly boundless. (Gardening also provides the perfect reason for many men to purchase a truck, a decision which might be otherwise difficult to defend.)

There are larger reasons why gardening is so deeply anchored in contemporary American life—reasons that are observed from some distance, but may be occasionally implied by practicing gardeners. Gardens often provide an experience of the passing of time and seasons for people whose lives and foodstuff supply are unchanging and climate-controlled. A garden tells the people who work it the time of year—something which is increasingly difficult to glean from a visit to the supermarket, where everything is in season (California or Florida season, that is) year-round. A vegetable garden is also a self-effacing work of decorative art, often undertaken for pleasure under the appearances of productive labor. A gardener may privately revel in the daily appearance of zucchini flowers or in the patterned rows of corn plants without ever being regarded as an aesthete, knowing that the squash and corn the garden yields are testimony to more obvious (if secondary) intentions.

## DISTRIBUTION
## OF FOODSTUFFS

*The places where people come to buy (and sell) foodstuffs have historically been centers of civic and community life. The very term "marketplace" conjures images of the intersection of social and commercial life that reflect back beyond American history to more ancient antecedents. If the modern American shopping mall has successfully replaced the city and small-town marketplace, it is because the mall has adapted key features of the marketplace, including its compactness, variety, and levels of activity. The so-called "food court" that has become the multi-venue eatery for many shopping malls completes this referential circle, and thus provides an element of familiarity for today's young people who may not have experienced a marketplace firsthand.*

What happens to the foodstuffs that are gathered or produced between the time they leave field or factory and the time they are cooked? Some homegrown foodstuffs may be distributed among family or neighbors as suggested above, but most are commercially marketed, a link in the food chain with particular cultural features. These features include the character of the places where foodstuffs are sold and the social life associated with them as well as foodstuffs that are region-specific in supply, demand, or mystique.

The places where people come to buy (and sell) foodstuffs have historically been centers of civic and community life. The very term "marketplace" conjures images of the intersection of social and commercial life that reflect back beyond American history to more ancient antecedents. If the modern American shopping mall has successfully replaced the city and small-town marketplace, it is because the mall has adapted key features of the marketplace, including its compactness, variety, and levels of activity. The so-called "food court" that has become the multi-venue eatery for many shopping malls completes this referential circle, and thus provides an element of familiarity for today's young people who may not have experienced a marketplace firsthand.

City or town markets do not tell the whole story of the foodstuff distribution, but they are a good place to start. Marketing, the activity that establishes and meaning and style of these places, is based in the pre-refrigeration era, when freshness was a meter of wholesomeness that had begun ticking before produce or meat were put on

*This food court at a shopping mall is an example of food following function—literally a mall of eateries. (Photo by Kay Danielson)*

daily display. Marketing was, and in some quarters still is, the art of knowing when as well as what to purchase. The divisions of the traditional marketplace are reflected in the departmental organization of most modern supermarkets, but having conquered the problem of seasonal supply, the supermarket provides a marketplace without the risks and opportunities that challenged purchasers of foodstuffs a generation ago.

The places where people buy foodstuffs today include a variety of facilities whose differences are defined more sharply by the prominence of the supermarket. Municipal or neighborhood stall markets, including those in Baltimore or Seattle's Pike Place Market,[3] to name just two, tend to be more frequently photographed today, and have entered the class of "scenic" places likely to be included on bus tours, but are more likely to be appreciated for the way they look than the foodstuff they sell. Stall markets, particularly those where multiple produce, meat, seafood, and/or bakery vendors continue to compete under the same roof, maintain a style of display and customer exchange that is natural to no other locale. The key element, invisible in contemporary photographs of these places, is knowledge shared between customer and vendor—knowledge of what the vendor sells and knowledge of each other. This is not to say that stall markets specialize in customer service, per se, but that they tend to work to the advantage of both vendor and customer when the customer knows what he or she wants, or wants to cook. The culture exerts itself when the vendor knows enough about what the customers are likely to be cooking to accommodate their special requests, without treating them as "special orders."

*This farmers' market, like many throughout the nation, is located at a permanent, covered, but open-air site in an urban downtown. (Photo by Kay Danielson)*

One characteristic of stall markets that attracts photographers is the aesthetic arrangement of produce, meat, or fish, each of which exhibits a pattern language that differs from the one practiced at the supermarket or neighborhood store. In Baltimore, at least, the special way that wares are displayed is traced by current stall operators to previous operators, many of whom are fathers, grandfathers, or other family members. When greens are in season they are piled high and deep, as if to accentuate their abundance. Out-of-season fruits, like cherries or pears in winter, are displayed with their wrappings barely turned back, in boxes that say they have come a long way. The development of a distinctive style in such a temporary medium is not an easy thing to do or maintain, given the ever-present risk that in such close quarters a too delicately balanced pyramid of oranges or helix of strawberry boxes will tumble onto the sawdust floor. Patrons who are judging each stand's produce for the most part on the basis of appearance find the display styles a natural, and to an extent, an expected element of

*Business is brisk at an outdoor farmers' market. (Photo by Kay Danielson)*

*Fruit vendors stack their wares for maximum eye-catching appeal. (Photo courtesy of Smithsonian Institution, Office of Folklife Programs)*

the merchant's appeal for business.

An interesting aspect of this presentation of wares is the importance of varying the displays, even when the foodstuffs being offered to customers are unchanged. The relative simplicity of the stall setup has traditionally accommodated seasonal changes in the produce or seafood being sold. Regular customers are invited to look closely by the vendor's requiring them to see each day's, or week's, display anew. Some vendors go to considerable lengths to secure game in season or exotic fruits and vegetables to "dress up" their displays, even if they continue to earn their living from foodstuffs more constant in supply.

Stall markets, of course, were the supermarkets of their generation—improving upon their forebears by putting a roof over an open market space or, in some cases, spatially consolidating a number of independent butcher shops, bakeries, and produce businesses. Of these small businesses, the seasonal produce stand deserves special attention as a fixture of lowgrade commerce in most parts of the country. The idea of eliminating the wholesaler in the purchase of foodstuffs has an eternal appeal to American consumers, and a flatbed wagon parked alongside a cornfield has a real advantage selling corn in season even if—and this is frequently the case—the corn being sold has not come from the adjacent field. Stopping at roadside stands is part of the traditional itinerary for Maryland vacationers headed to or from ocean resorts. The stands have made a number of adaptations to their high-volume, quick-transaction trade, but the more successful ones have managed to make improvements that do not substantially change the flatbed-at-the-edge-of-the-cornfield appearance and commercial style that is their identifying badge.

Other kinds of vendors hold special value for the people they serve largely due to

*Shoppers at Belair Market in Baltimore, Maryland, eye the catch of the day. (Photo by Roland L. Freeman)*

the first-name familiarity which develops between them. The distribution of home-cured "country" hams in Virginia and Maryland follows social trails blazed by family friendships and hunting buddyhood. Hams are sold in increasing numbers as the fall and new year's holidays approach, fragrant packages of scuffed newspapers changing hands at appointed places in parking lots and at neighborhood bars. The hams may not have customers' names on them in the backyard smokehouse, but by the time a ham is taken down its destination is arranged. The sale of game often follows similar channels, an interested individual securing some venison for the holidays by passing the word along through friends, trusting established social ties to deliver the desired foodstuff sight unseen.

Baltimore's arabbers, whose vending cries or "hollers" were referred to in Chapter Two, also rely upon familiarity with the customers along their neighborhood routes. Arabbers in earlier times served as the fingers of the city's foodstuff distribution service—extending the provision of fresh fruit, vegetables, fish, crabs, and oysters into those parts of the city not served by one of the five neighborhood stall markets. The arabbers have resisted recent attempts to bring their colorful horsecarts fully into the tourist orbit by stationing them at visible downtown locations, and have instead adapted to a more mobile clientele by specializing in local melons, peaches, and other crops available at low wholesale prices during the summer months.

Seasonal and regional availability of foodstuffs is the subject that comes to many minds as a contributing determinant, if not the definition, of American foodways. The subject has so long preoccupied those who have defined American regions or their culinary character that the disappearance of certain of the foodstuffs or their ex-

*The street vendors of Baltimore, Maryland, known as "arabbers," remain a vital and visible part of the city's produce distribution system. (Photo by Roland L. Freeman)*

panded distribution to national marketplaces has gone virtually unnoticed. When the Federal Writers' Project published *U.S. One: Maine to Florida* in 1938 as one of the first volumes in the American Guide Series, its tours editor, Katharine A. Kellock, bemoaned the passage of American epicureanism and the standards of excellence such cultivated and demanding tastes maintained in restaurant kitchens.[4] But the first chapter of the book, and the only one save a calendar of annual events along the highway to deal with the eastern seaboard as a whole, consisted of a detailed state-by-state description of local specialties for travelers to request en route. Mrs. Kellock supplied the following note at the end of the list:

> In the above list a few dishes appear in more than one state. Succotash, for example, is made of corn with any kind of fresh beans in one state; in a second it is made of corn with lima beans only; and in a third of corn with beans, okra, and tomatoes. It will be observed that most of the dishes are made of foods native to America; the best dishes of every land are those developed by native cooks from local products. Few American cooks are entirely successful in following French recipes and few French cooks can cook a typical American meal. A blighting influence on American cooking has been the attempt to impose French menus on the American people without an understanding of French cooking methods and the use of French ingredients.[5]

The same year a similar Eastern multi-state guide was published by the Writers' Project, *The Ocean Highway: New Brunswick, New Jersey to Jacksonville, Florida*. Mrs. Kellock wrote another state-by-state list of local culinary specialties, preceded by a brief statement:

The Ocean Highway country is famous as the land of good food; nature has supplied a wide variety of fine ingredients and the inhabitants know well how to use them. Recipes are handed down from generation to generation, along with the family plate and portraits. Mention of special dishes provides a useful conversational wedge everywhere along the route and has been known to create firm friendships. Only a word of praise for a good meal is needed in a hotel to bring service that money can not buy.

Of all the pleasures offered by the coastal country, food stands at the head of the list.[6]

What is notable about these statements is their premise: that the best American food is prepared by people who make use of "native" ingredients in preparation of foods passed down within their families. In an interview I conducted with Mrs. Kellock in 1979, she pointed out that the counsel given to travelers to ask for local foods was as much intended to cultivate a lasting demand for them as to make conversation or "create firm friendships." In addition to identifying the natural conditions which provided the environments for the varied regional foodstuffs along the East Coast, the guidebooks were meant to stave off what Mrs. Kellock perceived as the homogenization of taste in restaurant food, and particularly the rising fashion of "French" food.

It was Mrs. Kellock's assumption, and it has been many others' since, that local or regional foodstuffs are the source for local or regional foods, and that as tastes become more cosmopolitan, demand for local specialties falls—taking with it the impetus to maintain production or gathering of regionally specific fruit, vegetables, or fish. But advances in packing and shipping technology Mrs. Kellock could not have foreseen have made regional foodstuffs nationally available, and dramatically altered local supply and demand in the process. In fact, since the 1940s the loss of distinctive regional foodstuffs—wild berries and other native edible wild plants, varieties of fish, game animals—has been fairly uniform nationwide. Attention given to dwindling supplies of key limes, persimmons, or Chincoteague oysters similarly increases demand for these foodstuffs nationwide, as American consumers who have tired of the French food the guidebooks decry have sought them out. And the rarer a foodstuff is, the more likely it is to fetch a higher profit being exported rather than being used in traditional ways within its native region.

All of which is to say that there are more varieties of fresh oysters available at the Grand Central Station's Oyster Bar in New York City than anywhere on the East Coast; the finest-quality aged beef is to be had in big city restaurants on either coast rather than a steakhouse near the stockyards in Kansas City; and the lion's share of soft crabs from the soft-crab capital of the world, Crisfield, Maryland, are shipped not to the towns of the Chesapeake, but to Tokyo.

But Mrs. Kellock need not have feared. Even if the quality and price of Gulf Coast shrimp or DelMarVa cantaloupes is not much different in those regions that produce them from the big-city restaurants that procure them, regional foodstuffs persist. Restaurants may corner the redfish market, but after the wave of the trend has crested the familiarity and popularity of stuff gathered close to home re-emerges, and those households that never really got away from dry-cured ham or crabapples will return

*Regional foodstuffs persist. Restaurants may corner the redfish market, but after the wave of the trend has crested the familiarity and popularity of stuff gathered close to home re-emerges, and those households that never really got away from dry-cured ham or crabapples will return to them. What makes regional foodstuffs regional is neither the demand nor the supply, but the extent to which a foodstuff is woven into the culture of a community— Sunday dinner, the peanut festival, a suitcase full of red pepper.*

to them. What makes regional foodstuffs regional is neither the demand nor the supply, but the extent to which a foodstuff is woven into the culture of a community—Sunday dinner, the peanut festival, a suitcase full of red pepper.

## COOKERY

It is not surprising that cookery should hold such a central position in American foodways, or that its prominence should overshadow some of the other elements of food and culture this book has presented as of equal importance. The prominence is deserved on two accounts—the high respect that is accorded the person who cooks, and cooks well; and the almost magical forces involved in the turning of foodstuffs into food.

Magic is often identified as the active force behind occurrences for which there is no observable cause but an observable effect. So it is with cookery, much of which takes place in dark places like ovens, at speeds too slow to be observed by the naked eye, according to chemical processes difficult to understand or predict except in error. No wonder that the person or persons who orchestrate the fragile chemistry of cookery are objects of admiration and wonderment. Who has not heard of, or perhaps been subject to, such common bedevilments as "can't make gravy," or "cakes don't turn out," or "dumplings are like lead"? These are not always reported as technical shortcomings or failure to grasp a simple trick of the trade; a great many people, including a goodly number of otherwise competent and confident cooks, believe an element of the cookery repertoire to be beyond their grasp, accepted as among the many things that cannot be known about cooking.

Because the subject of cookery has generated such a massive body of description, instruction, and diagnostic self-help, it would serve no useful purpose to review its

*An apple taken from a bag that claims that the fruit has been washed is a foodstuff; polished lightly against a shirtsleeve or washed again, it is a food.*

**An apple is a foodstuff; peeled, sliced, and baked into a pie, it becomes a food. (Photo by Kay Danielson)**

scope and cultural aspects. But some observations on the culture of cookery within the context of the larger process outlined here may be in order.

First of all, cookery includes such a wide variety of method and technique that no description of how foodstuffs are changed by it could adequately cover all examples. What is central, and perhaps irreducible, is the humanizing aspect of the cookery process, which alters the perception of the foodstuff in question from a thing of the natural order to a thing of the human order. This alteration is almost universally brought about by the physical processing of the foodstuff, often in ways that seem wholly symbolic. Consider, for example, these minimalist cases: A cucumber is a foodstuff; peeled, cut into pieces, or its skin serrated with the tines of a fork, it is a food. An apple taken from a bag that claims that the fruit has been washed is a foodstuff; polished lightly against a shirtsleeve or washed again, it is a food. In virtually every instance, eating something without altering it in some way presupposes that the person handing it to you has already done so.

The commonly observed process of washing raw foods before eating them is wholly cultural; all parties to our upbringing—doctors, schoolteachers, parents— instruct us to wash everything we eat, or trust that the people who offer food to us have done so. But the utter uniformity of this processing places health imperatives within the larger culture of cooking, rather than subjecting cooking to the imperative of health.

The notion of cookery as cultural processing applies to foods as well as foodstuffs. Leftovers are routinely turned into other foods, rather than reconstituted as themselves: mashed potatoes are converted to pancakes; leftover roast meat is served cold in sandwiches or chopped and recooked into barbecue. Many of the customs associated with polite table manners or household tidiness are similarly minimal, symbolic touches that transfer a food from one dish to another, from one size of portion to another, from the container it came in to a household container. The more formal the occasion the farther the distance between the natural and the civilized world will be expanded in the kitchen and at the dinner table—by transferring salad dressing from its storebought bottle into a little cruet, taking the wrapper off the butter, pouring beer into glasses. These touches seldom disguise the source of the food (homemade, storebought), but they represent a symbolic shedding of one identity and adoption of a new one. Things are changed from the world of goods to the world of the table, where the salad dressing "belongs," for the moment at least, solely to the meal in which it appears.

Chapter One described the social circumstances of a cook's apprenticeship. Beyond being able to put these skills individually into practice, the role of cook involves a coordination of household tasks that may be more challenging than a simple inventory might indicate. Suppose, for example, that in addition to cooking four or five different dishes, you are asked to have them all ready to serve at the same instant. This job requires a generalist, but a cook may just as often be called upon to specialize—to produce an unusually demanding piece of culinary work for a special occasion, knowing in advance that if he or she succeeds the request is likely to be repeated.

In examples provided in earlier chapters a cook may be designated according to criteria that have little to do with training or experience. The custom of men cooking foods prepared outdoors is accompanied in North Carolina by the belief that women

*Magic is often identified as the active force behind occurrences for which there is no observable cause but an observable effect. So it is with cookery, much of which takes place in dark places like ovens, at speeds too slow to be observed by the naked eye, according to chemical processes difficult to understand or predict except in error. No wonder that the person or persons who orchestrate the fragile chemistry of cookery are objects of admiration and wonderment.*

*The more formal the occasion, the farther the distance between the natural and the civilized world will be expanded in the kitchen and at the dinner table—by transferring salad dressing from its storebought bottle into a little cruet, taking the wrapper off the butter, pouring beer into glasses. These touches seldom disguise the source of the food (homemade, storebought), but they represent a symbolic shedding of one identity and adoption of a new one. Things are changed from the world of goods to the world of the table, where the salad dressing "belongs," for the moment at least, solely to the meal in which it appears.*

Assigning cooking chores by gender is common. The larger the enterprise, the more public and outdoors the cookery, the more likely a man will be in charge. This fact is made all the more striking by the countering fact that, with the exception of large restaurant kitchens, most American cooks are women, and that even in a society whose career and social demands on men and women are changing rapidly, today's men of marriageable age have usually received no more training in the culinary arts at home than their fathers did in theirs. A given household situation—parents with two jobs or night classes, single working parents, and so on—may require a boy's learning to cook, but the association of gender and cookery appears to remain consistent.

*Some rake coals to stoke up the barbecue pit while others "direct" from the sidelines. (Photo courtesy of Smithsonian Institution, Office of Folklife Programs)*

*Cooks toil over barbecued chicken at a church social. The larger the food event, the more open and public its venue, the more likely it is that those in charge will be male—even in contemporary America, with its changing gender roles. (Photo by Kay Danielson)*

"keep the meat from breathing," and exists elsewhere minus this belief. Assigning cooking chores by gender is common. The larger the enterprise, the more public and outdoors the cookery, the more likely a man will be in charge. This fact is made all the more striking by the countering fact that, with the exception of large restaurant kitchens, most American cooks are women, and that even in a society whose career and social demands on men and women are changing rapidly, today's men of marriageable age have usually received no more training in the culinary arts at home than their fathers did in theirs. A given household situation—parents with two jobs or night classes, single working parents, and so on—may require a boy's learning to cook, but the association of gender and cookery appears to remain consistent.

Folklorist Tom Adler has observed changing gender territoriality in the household kitchen which may assign a particular meal—most commonly Sunday breakfast—to a male head of household, and reaffirms the assignment of outdoor cookery to men. Claude Lévi-Strauss had asserted earlier that boiling is a female enterprise and roasting (or other fire-on-food processes) is a male enterprise.[7] Such theories about why gender roles break down as they do usually lead to the designation of certain cooking (or household) tasks as "women's work," or the designation of social territory as the male or female province. The close observation of these designations make theories like Lévi-Strauss's difficult to support in the face of changing technologies and social roles which make assignments such as these less clear-cut and consistently observed.[8]

Cooking is itself part work, sport, and performance, involving risk-taking and improvising as frequently as precision and skilled routine. The performance aspects of cookery derive in part from a few somewhat varied opportunities to witness cooking *as* performance. Cooking demonstrations, including those occasionally staged at department or grocery stores, serve as models, as do more recent videotaped instructional programs or television broadcasts that highlight technique over choice of foodstuffs or foods. The parts of the cookery process that are pre-selected for such performances, and thereby identified as the key moments in the process, are generally of two kinds— those which involve the combination of ingredients, and those which require some special hand skill—such as frying food in a wok, kneading bread dough, or stuffing a roast. The cumulative repetition of this formula creates a series of pivotal moments in which all previous efforts, presumably including the gathering of necessary ingredients and their proper measurement, may be lost in an instant of carelessness or miscalculation.

*Contestants at a Bandolero Chili cook-off wield knives and spices and whet appetites.*

For sheer artistry and showmanship, however, few performances match the routine presented at state or county fairs by sellers of combination slicing/chopping/shredding machines. These gadgets, occasionally pitched on television, never perform so beautifully in less experienced hands, but the wonderment of oddly-shaped pieces of vegetables and fruit produced in lightning speed, along with a humorous sales speech, is often too much for fairgoers, who buy the appliances as a tribute to the performance as well as a useful addition to a kitchen gadgetry collection.

Although many actual cooking performances spotlight technique, the promise of a step-by-step recipe generally calms the cook who fears a critical ingredient or procedure may have been overlooked. Recipes are the established currency of cooking, yet even the most avid collector of cookbooks, magazine clip-out formulae, and handwritten secrets participates in a system of social courtesies that limits the use and usefulness of written recipes while accumulating more and more of them. Even cooks committed to the continual improvement of their skills find that the established preferences of the people they feed leave little opportunity for experiment, and that few experiments receive fair judgment from first-time eaters. Therefore, recipes that haven't found their way into a cook's active repertoire by early adulthood are likely to serve as a more reliable indication of what kinds of things the cook might wish to prepare if the opportunity presented itself than what he or she regularly prepares for others to eat. The dis-

*Cookbooks are perennially popular. (Photo by Kay Danielson)*

tinction being made here is somewhat analogous to the division of storytelling or musical repertoires into active and inactive parts, the two representing in sum the total learned ability of the tradition-bearer.

The custom of asking the cook who prepared a dish to furnish a copy of the recipe leads to a compiled cookbook that is a more useful record of the acquaintances of the recipient of the recipes than his or her tastes or cooking preferences. Asking for a recipe is a gesture demanded in situations where praise is generally directed toward the cook, and chiming in may not reflect the true judgment or tastes of each recipient of a copy. But, like Christmas cards from distant and seldom-seen relatives, recipe cards once received are difficult to throw away. Various recipes, whether clipped from newspapers or gathered from acquaintances, often find their way to a drawer or filecard box, where they may come to constitute a barely organized social register of a cook and homemaker.

A few years ago I purchased a looseleaf notebook at a second-hand bookstore that turned out to be just such a document. Its contents reveal how advice for the future

*A recipe file may serve as a catch-all for coupons, warranty and instruction booklets, household tips, and family heirlooms. Though uniquely personal and private, it is casually stored within easy reach in one of the most public spaces of the home—the kitchen. (Photo by Kay Danielson)*

*Meat cutters and butchers display their occupational skills at the 1971 Festival of American Folklife. (Photo courtesy of Smithsonian Institution, Office of Folklife Programs)*

and recollection of the past are overlapping enterprises, and how among so many other duties the cook/homemaker is responsible for maintaining both branches of wisdom.

The notebook is an inexpensive black looseleaf binder, its cover sprung from over-stuffing. Although there are thirty pages of looseleaf paper held in place by the note-book's two metal rings nothing is written or pasted on them; the notebook's contents are folded newspaper and magazine clippings stuck into the binder on either side of the blank paper. Among the clippings are recipes for dozens of varieties of cookies and cakes, the owner's manual for a Westinghouse "Completely Balanced" refrigera-tor, and handwritten 3x5" index cards for "buttermilk rolls," "red earth cake," and "clean iron." Amid the file cards are handwritten pieces of paper—some railway stationery—with untitled cooking instructions for casserole dishes, and two more (different) recipes for buttermilk rolls. Each of these has a name written on the re-verse side in a different hand. Tucked in the back is a booklet of Atlas fruit jar labels, a 28-page Betty Crocker Bisquick Party Book, and the holiday entertainment section of the Baltimore *Sun* for December 12, 1941. Among the booklets is a 3x3" square of wrapping paper with a printed baby shower motif and a graded elementary school exercise (A).

Looking through the notebook, which offers numerous clues but never names its owner, is an enlightening but unsettling experience. The enlightening part is the wholeness of the thing—the overlap of holiday recipes and souvenirs, recipes gath-ered from people and from the local newspaper, and household information. The book is unsettling because it juxtaposes privacy and openness—obviously never in-tended to be read by others, yet most likely kept in an easy-to-reach place in a Balti-

*Like Christmas cards from distant and seldom-seen relatives, recipe cards once received are difficult to throw away.*

more kitchen for years. If the book were the only document of its kind from its era there is much that we might learn from it, and without corroboration, much we might mistakenly conclude. If there were one dollar for every cookie recipe tucked away in every repository of this kind the national debt might be halved, yet the per capita consumption of cookies in America probably does not equal the per cook collection of cookie (and buttermilk roll) recipes. Archaeologists will know a great deal about the kitchens of the late twentieth century because the operating manual for every major appliance purchased during that period is maintained in each household's kitchen repository.

But beyond this, a cook's records are the records of how regularly social worlds—special occasions, friends, family—and the world of food—recipes, instructions, mementoes—converge, and how much the records of one world stand for the other.

## DISTRIBUTION OF FOODS

*Special food items, like these made by Sweet Apple Farm, are a popular gift. (Photo by Kay Danielson)*

Not all cooks perform their magic in the home, and those who do so exclusively may not channel their work into meals. This category looks at what happens to food in between the time it is cooked and the time it is eaten—the distribution of food in gifts and in commercial venues.

Gifts of food are more numerous and more varied than the gifts of produce or other foodstuffs already discussed, and include offerings that convey sentiments deeply rooted in community culture. Most households that bake Christmas cookies intentionally prepare more of them than they can eat. The disposal of this surplus accommodates both in-house hospitality (a plate kept stocked for guests who drop in) and plates made up for giving to neighbors and relatives. So common is this practice that the greeting-card industry markets empty containers, marked with holiday colors and decoration, to accommodate baked gifts. However, the use of a disposable container for such gifts short-circuits another custom which observes that an empty plate may not be returned to its original owner, and that social reciprocity is served only when the gift recipient becomes the donor of similar goods.

Other gifts of food that enjoy enhanced popularity around the Christmas holiday are homemade jellies and jams, for which—again—special Christmas packaging is sold. Unlike most other gifts of food, in order to enjoy these it is not necessary to eat them. The donor's selection of a fruit or recipe that provides a deeply colored or translucent jelly and the recipient's appreciation of it as a thing of beauty completes the gesture. Eating, and reporting to the donor that the jam or jelly was delicious, is almost superfluous.

Not all home-canned goods are foods, of course, and many, like cold-packed toma-

**The Ozark Mountain Smokehouse offers a variety of locally smoked meats. (Photo by Kay Danielson)**

Other gifts of food that enjoy enhanced popularity around the Christmas holiday are homemade jellies and jams, for which special Christmas packaging is sold. Unlike most other gifts of food, in order to enjoy these it is not necessary to eat them. The donor's selection of a fruit or recipe that provides a deeply colored or translucent jelly and the recipient's appreciation of it as a thing of beauty completes the gesture. Eating, and reporting to the donor that the jam or jelly was delicious, is almost superfluous.

**Besides providing delicious tastes to be enjoyed at some future date, home canners create visual delights for the present. (Photo courtesy of Smithsonian Institution, Office of Folklife Programs)**

toes or corn, require cooking rather than simple heating before being ready to eat. But especially among those canned goods that *are* ready-to-eat there is a highly evolved aesthetic that guides the production of pickles and other mixed fruit and vegetable preserves. Cooks who can produce a matrix of baby onions in a half-pint jar, or create alternating stripes of green and red in a canned olive salad, follow an aesthetic custom that is recognized for its artistry in state and county fairs but seldom elsewhere. The objects produced in aesthetic canning are even less likely to be eaten than a pretty jar of jelly, and represent an unusually high degree of devotion to craft beyond that which is required to produce a wholesome and table-worthy jar of food. Many canners who produce these special effects in a jar, the difficulty of which may be compared to a ship in a bottle, maintain their own canning shelves in arrangements that play the color of one food against another, rather than following the traditional grocery-store classifications of fruits in one place, vegetables in another. In fact, just as gardening provides a useful cover for aesthetic indulgences, home canning underscores food's attractiveness.

Another common food gift is the funeral casserole—food prepared by neighbors of a household in which a family member living at the house has recently died. This custom is widely practiced across regional and ethnic lines, and sends a number of complementary messages about neighborly relations, bereavement, and the importance of food. A cooked dish brought to the home by a neighbor says, among other things, that the grieving family will not want for lack of food; that their absorption in the emotions of the moment is appropriate, and the cook of the household should not be required to spend time cooking for his or her guests; and that the neighbor wishes to express feelings of sympathy, but understands why the occasion must be reserved for the immediate family. It is interesting to note that unlike person-to-person gifts, food given at the time of a neighbor's death is given household to household, and generally eschews the types of food ordinarily given—cakes, pies, and cookies, which perhaps convey cheerier sentiments than the occasion calls for. More common are bread, meat, cheese, salads, and other foods that need little preparation for a meal, and may be set out for family and guests as the need arises.

The cultural aspects of the distribution of food considered thus far are all cradled in social custom, with some commercial accommodation. Much of this category, how-

ever, is nakedly instinctual, and increasingly more so. The study of how food is distributed leads directly to the behavior Calvin Trillin termed "looking for something to eat," and the campaigns waged by food vendors of all types to ambush the search party en route. Given the growing numbers of Americans who eat two or more meals outside the home, or prepared by cooks outside the home, the notion of "home cooking" has taken on a mercantile meaning at odds with prior connotations. The interpenetration of the professional food industry and the American household has shaped a new reality that partially obscures long-held tenets about restaurants and "eating out."

It may be difficult for people to recall the era, which appeared to end about twenty years ago, when a family's eating a meal away from home was an exception to household rule ordinarily prompted by such extraordinary circumstances as vacation or a broken water main. Restaurants in this (not very) faraway time were regarded by married people with children as places where courting couples went to be alone, salesmen or other unfortunate professional travelers were forced to dine, and adolescents squandered their allowance and appetite. Restaurants were places where some part of the family unit might indulge themselves—Mom and Dad celebrating an anniversary or an out-of-town uncle treating the kids—but the normative family ate its normative meals in its normative home. The very idea that families should eat home-cooked meals every night except in extreme emergencies seems hopelessly antique today. Yet it reflects a prescribed role for the home cook that varied little in the first half of this century,

*In times gone by, the vast majority of American meals were prepared at home on the likes of this cast-iron stove. (Photo by Kay Danielson)*

*It may be difficult for people to recall the era, which appeared to end about twenty years ago, when a family's eating a meal away from home was an exception to household rule ordinarily prompted by such extraordinary circumstances as vacation or a broken water main. Restaurants in this (not very) faraway time were regarded by married people with children as places where courting couples went to be alone, salesmen or other unfortunate professional travelers were forced to dine, and adolescents squandered their allowance and appetite. Restaurants were places where some part of the family unit might indulge themselves—Mom and Dad celebrating an anniversary or an out-of-town uncle treating the kids, but the normative family ate its normative meals in its normative home.*

and a degree of pride in both the conscientious exercise of the homemaker's craft and the quality of home cooking that remained unchallenged.

These generalities are not without exceptions, and some of them point up directions for change in our time that an analyst of the hospitality industries might have foreseen. Aside from occasions (food events) that brought the family out of the house at suppertime for social as well as culinary reasons—church suppers, potluck dinners, organizational picnics—a few traditionally favorite foods were, and still are, regarded as better cooked outside the home. These include barbecue, fried fish, and pizza. The fact that all three may be regarded as somewhat less healthful than standard home kitchen fare may explain why in most households, even those where barbecue was commonly loved, they were less frequently brought home than the eaters in the house might have liked. When they were, it was often on a night that offered even a slight pretext for a night off from cooking—payday, for example. And few cooks willingly conceded the turf to a professional kitchen, experimenting with home techniques and ingredients in attempts to approximate the characteristics of the eatery product.

Such efforts always failed, not because the secrets of barbecue are ultimately beyond home divination, but because the appeal of the food was at least in part based upon non-culinary factors. A dinner of fried fish, hush puppies, french fried potatoes, and cole slaw cooked at home did not come in a box, with little containers holding each food, a plastic fork, and a sanitary-sealed moist towelette.

There are real reasons, of course, why some foods *are* better when cooked away from home—commercial pizza ovens operate at higher temperatures than their kitchen equivalents, some barbecued meats cook and taste better when prepared in sides, slabs, and other quantities beyond the measure of the home charcoal grill, and deep frying dinner for a family of four (assuming all plan to eat at the same time) overtaxes even the largest home-scale fryer. But these reasons, and the nostalgic appeal of restaurant meals recalled from courtship days and other special occasions, represent only the foot the food industry kept in the door of the American household until the 1960s. Increasingly, partly as the result of the proliferation and improvement of away-from-home cooking and the impact of the automobile on American culture, the places outside the home where food was served gained in appeal and acceptance. Americans, especially young Americans, began to frequent them in growing numbers, and the hospitality industry seized the opportunity to break down the remaining barriers between the home and the commercial kitchen.

The resultant mix of eat-out, take-home, micro-reheat, and made-from-scratch meals in the American household has taken the search for "something to eat" beyond the bounds of the homeplace. Now, rather than judging food eaten out against homecooked standards, people engage in skilled taste-testing of comparable foods from a variety of venues against each other. A hamburger, taco, pizza, or even a salad prepared at home is likely to be judged against a commercial standard, rather than the reverse, which might have been the norm twenty years ago. The mystique that surrounds the most popular eateries takes on characteristics of the arguments about

*Many Americans now eat take-out fast food on a regular basis. (Photo by Kay Danielson)*

*Bill and Sue Williams relax for a moment in Cheshire Books, their bookstore-cum-bakery in Little Rock, Arkansas. (Photo by Kay Danielson)*

regional foodstuffs: when in Chicago, eat pizza, when in Kansas City, Arthur Bryant's barbecue. Associations of places and foods have always mixed foodstuffs believed to be only in local supply, commercial venues of reputedly impressive scale, grandeur, or eccentricity, and the kind of local specialties Katharine Kellock listed in the FWP guidebooks. But the issue now is not whether restaurants adequately convey the essence of local home cooking (via local foodstuffs, local recipes, and so on), but whether an eatery **stands for** or represents local culinary traditions more successfully than home cooking.

The culture of restaurants and other eateries involves more than food. The art and science of getting a good table at a big-city restaurant is the subject of much advice-giving and conjecture, not only word-of-mouth, but in magazine essays that describe how power and prestige are showcased in table assignments at Antoine's or the Tavern on the Green. The attachments people develop for particular commercial foods overshadow the appeal of home cooking Perry Como eternalized in his "Home for the Holidays"; long drives or high-risk mailings characterize the out-of-town demand for Cincinnati chili[9] or New York bagels. Just as significant is the way that people talk about these foods, and the fact that the audiences who listen to such tales can, in fact, measure the teller's superlatives by trying the favored food themselves. This opportunity is somewhat reduced when the food being praised is "my mom's biscuits"; hence commercially available food lends itself to developing mystique more readily. People are more likely to believe praise for a food they know they may have the chance to try for themselves than for one which will come their way only with an invitation to someone's parents' home for supper.

*Bakeries combine well with any enterprise— here, a bed-and-breakfast in the Arkansas Ozarks. (Photo by Kay Danielson)*

*Now, rather than judging food eaten out against homecooked standards, people engage in skilled taste-testing of comparable foods from a variety of venues against each other. A hamburger, taco, pizza, or even a salad prepared at home is likely to be judged against a commercial standard, rather than the reverse, which might have been the norm twenty years ago.*

This also helps to explain why restaurant guides may be more reliable indicators these days of regional patterns in American food than cookbooks, and why ethnic restaurants are important commercial points of entry for recently immigrated peoples. There are two different senses in which ethnic restaurants—those labeled by their proprietors or perceived by the customers as linked in some way with an ethnic or nationality group—display traditionality. The first is common to restaurants as businesses that offer recently-immigrated groups a rung on the American economic ladder. Creating and managing a successful restaurant in a new place is a challenge for anyone, of course, but for the newly arrived, this kind of business offers some distinct advantages: cooking skills are already developed and are not linked to language or other cultural fluency; a restaurant may provide an opportunity to keep one or more families together, providing roles for all family members; and the business provides familiar food at low cost to those who operate it.

The second way in which an ethnic restaurant is culturally identified is in the relationship between the cook and the patrons—a sliding social scale that pinpoints the use of ethnicity as well as the ethnic "authenticity" of the food. Some relationships on this scale:

◆ members of an ethnic group serving primarily other members of the same ethnic group: the kind of place restaurant critics and anthropologists seek out, where common culture maintains standards of authenticity; markers include outsiders' vague sense of not being welcome (a true four-star) or language gap

◆ members of an ethnic group serving mixed patrons: a restaurant that may be perceived by ethnic patrons as one kind of place, by outsiders as another, as in a kosher delicatessen, which serves as a source of certifiably appropriate food for one community and as a sandwich shop for patrons-at-large

◆ members of an ethnic group serving primarily non-members: examples include the Chinese-American restaurant, which serves a version of ethnic-based food to a non-ethnically identified clientele, or Cincinnati chili parlors—owned and operated by Greek-American families, serving a version of Greek spaghetti-with-meat without ethnic identification[10]

◆ non-members of an ethnic group serving "ethnic" food to general patrons: as in a chain taco restaurant that interprets (from the outside) ethnic food for general patrons; no claim of authenticity

*An array of bulk fresh spices greets the visitor to a health-food grocery store. (Photo by Kay Danielson; courtesy of Beans & Grains & Things)*

*This colored box label c. 1970 uses natural images to suggest the product's freshness. (Photo courtesy of Vandegrift-Williams Farms, Inc.)*

In addition, ethnic restaurants may function as gathering points for ethnic communities and educators of public taste and attitude.

The marketing of foods—their commercial distribution—is by nature counterpoised to elements of tradition and cultural continuity in American foodways. No matter how purposefully dieticians try to change contemporary food habits, companies that produce, package, and sell foods have managed to dominate the point of purchase. The accoutrements of the commerce in food are themselves increasingly appreciated as things of beauty, independent of their ability to render nature into art.[11] The depictions of food that form the symbolic vocabulary for jar and can labels, produce crate stickers, logos, advertising characters, and television commercials travel between realistic and stylistic points of view, creating an alternating current of association and correspondence. Two concentric circles are the American symbol for donut; a larger circle with a few randomly placed dots means pizza. Cherries are differentiated from other round fruit by a stylized stem; pictures of peaches show two small leaves at the stem point. Beer and root beer are stylized by a perpetual surface of foam, but bubbles rising from the surface signify liquor. The natural shape of wheat, peanuts, or tomatoes may be used to identify processed foods made from these foodstuffs, but the animals from which processed meats derive are never depicted.

*From the Pillsbury Dough Boy to Tony the Tiger, a whole host of characters born on the drawing-board of the advertising world plies the American public with food. (Photo courtesy of the Museum of Modern Mythology, San Francisco, California)*

This graphic vocabulary only hints at the degree of sophistication in food packages that purposefully mix the purest abstract qualities of color, texture, and contrast. Which means candy, of course. To grasp the variety and subtlety of the messages food can communicate, and how its commercial distribution expresses a code of product attributes, simply look over the candy counter at a neighborhood grocery store. The taxonomies are themselves complex—candy, candy bar, candies, gum, bubble gum, mint, breath mint, caramel, taffy, chocolate, edible apparel (candy necklaces, bracelets, shoelaces, and wax teeth)—and veer frequently into neighboring territory—cough drops, baking ingredients (cake decorations, baking chocolate, maraschino cherries), and breakfast cereals. Color and flavor cut across these categories, and combine them into types which change form and re-emerge as new mer-

*The candy counter shows complex taxonomies, even while proclaiming itself "food as toy."*
*(Photo by Kay Danielson)*

*Cereal packagers try to appeal to the public's taste buds, nutritional knowledge, and sense of fun at the same time.*
*(Photo by Kay Danielson)*

chandise on a seasonal basis. Adults may seek out their favorite amid the clutter of new and unfamiliar things, but children revel in that which is new or most improbably hybridized. Knowing about the latest thing in candy, and developing an interesting mix of situational favorites (no single brand or variety will do) represents not only the mastery of the vocabulary, but also the ability to generate an image, a style.

Candy is food as toy, the ammunition with which to return fire in the ongoing parent-child struggle over playing with food. Some notes about nonnutritive uses of food are offered in the next section of this chapter, but much of the play behavior associated with food has to do not with the food itself, but the packaging, which is proper to the distribution of food rather than its consumption. This play behavior is most often part of the culture that develops informally and is sustained traditionally around a food, rather than the specific created or guided intention of the producer. The craft uses of oatmeal boxes, gum-wrapper chains, and coffee-can insectariums all help sell the product, as does the provision of toys or other objects in breakfast cereal boxes.

Proof-of-purchase offers and coupon clipping, injected with the right amount of enthusiasm and social structure (clubs, exchanges, collectors) becomes a sport that turns the human vocation of looking for something to eat into a sport unrelated to the food products being acquired. Sending in proofs of purchase and a few dollars for a t-shirt, pencil case, or other product with the logo or other advertising image of a food product on it is, for the consumer, a way of embellishing the culture of food and, for the manufacturer, an advertising dream come true.

Here, as we in Ohio used to say—with some commercial encouragement—the rubber meets the road. The observation and regulation of what people eat, how much they eat, how they eat it, how quickly they eat it, with sufficient or insufficient chews before swallowing, is a social science of great sophistication and particularity. Yet while the caloric and nutritional content of what people eat is the standard measure of health and well-being, strategies to change food habits have generally looked to food selection, rather than eating customs, as targets for reform.[12] Perhaps the thinking is that once foods have been purchased and the preparation of a meal is underway the consequences of its consumption have been determined.

That this is not necessarily so is one of several less obvious cultural variables in this last step of the foodways process. Others include the number and timing of meals, the degree of individual or group-based creativity brought to bear on the eating enterprise, customs linking the serving of food with occasion and assigned status of family roles, and both non-consumptive and nonnutritive uses of food.

A general statistical measure such as "calories consumed per twenty-four-hour period" immediately summons a host of cultural considerations, including what Amy Shuman has termed the "rhetoric of portions."[13] Shuman focuses upon the management of hospitality and food supply in social situations where custom recommends accepting food when one is not hungry and refusing food when one is. Other customs having to do with the distribution of food, particularly when it is in short supply, reveal status orders within households that are culturally based but seldom made explicit or otherwise plain. Edna Lewis, who grew up in the mountains of western Maryland, described in an interview I conducted with her in 1979 the patterns of deference observed in her home in lean and full years. According to Mrs. Lewis, when there was not enough food to go around she would serve the largest portion to her husband, and reserve the smallest for herself, giving the children amounts in-between, according to their size. Her husband would then divide some of his food among the children. As Mrs. Lewis explained it, the intention was to provide first for the breadwinner, without whose strength and ability to work no food would reach the table, then to divide the rest among the children, saving only a symbolic portion for herself. This pattern is so frequently repeated that it seems almost axiomatic in its practice, but what it reveals is a merging of practical and social concerns that characterize the place of food in culture.

More broadly, the organization of meals reflects customary understandings of food groups and the times of day when eating is appropriate that have virtually nothing to do with the physiobiology of hunger. To a great extent, it is the social impulse rather than the coincidence of hunger that determines when people eat. The high value we

*The social impulse rather than the coincidence of hunger determines when people eat. The high value we place on eating together is reflected in the lengths to which busy households go to find a common supper time and the social stigma placed on eating alone, particularly at holidays. When we say that someone we know should not "be alone at Thanksgiving," we mean that the Thanksgiving meal is not one that should be eaten alone. Work schedules and other non-social factors in the arrangement of eating times generally follow custom, rather than constrain it. Some have suggested that the triad of breakfast, lunch, and supper expresses our culture's magical adherence to the number three; indeed, the number of occasions during an average day when eating is appropriate or common suggests that the identification of only three meals per day is really the identification of three domestic food events per day.*

place on eating together is reflected in the lengths to which busy households go to find a common supper time and the social stigma placed on eating alone, particularly at holidays. When we say that someone we know should not "be alone at Thanksgiving," we mean that the Thanksgiving meal is not one that should be eaten alone. Work schedules and other non-social factors in the arrangement of eating times generally follow custom, rather than constrain it. Some have suggested that the triad of breakfast, lunch, and supper expresses our culture's magical adherence to the number three; indeed, the number of occasions during an average day when eating is appropriate or common suggests that the identification of only three meals per day is really the identification of three domestic food events per day.

The proliferation of eating occasions for people who follow an ordinary work or school schedule may not be so recent a phenomenon, but the current names for these times is a modern, and not altogether stable vocabulary. Coffee breaks and after-school and bedtime snacks designate both times of day and eating occasions, while the term "brunch" refers in common usage not only to a time of day, but to a certain level of sophistication associated with a meal otherwise known as "a late breakfast" among humbler folk. Eating is so widely accepted as a complement to all activities that it is permitted except where posted—the sole exception perhaps being the dead of night, when refrigerator raids are seen as clandestine affairs to be kept secret.

When "approved" mealtimes actually begin, and at what point the foods associated with each become appropriate, is an even more contentious matter. The definitive

**This restaurant serving mixed patrons specializes in French and Swiss food—though it has adopted the new American meal designation of "brunch." (Photo by Kay Danielson)**

standard, of course, is the time when a particular meal ceases to be served at the local eatery, as in the 10:30 a.m. cut-off for breakfast at McDonald's. But the merging of menus for lunch and dinner at many establishments, including McDonald's, means that the day is divided into two unequal parts—breakfast and non-breakfast. In this light, restaurants that feature breakfast at all hours are not so much leveling social customs having to do with appropriate foods at appropriate times but, by permitting exceptions, reinforcing them. Why breakfast and all other meals are mutually exclusive is a troublesome question, made more so by other linguistic confusions includ-

ing the relative interchangeability of the terms "dinner" and "supper" for an evening meal and "dinner" and "lunch" for a midday meal. It is as if, in a literal sense, our culture wishes to say that there is no difference between these two meals, but that breakfast, long the distant underdog among favored meals, is at the margins of social and culinary life. Calling it "the most important meal of the day" even further reduces the prospect of anyone's looking forward to it, and is about as positively persuasive as telling a child that of all the food on his plate the brussels sprouts are the best for him. If this is so, why would any restaurant want to serve breakfast all day?

The closest we can come to answers to these questions is to look at the three main meals of the day in terms of not only the foods associated with each but also the time of day they occur. In this sense, breakfast may more accurately be defined as the meal that we eat when we get up, no matter what time of day that happens to be. Lunch (or dinner) and supper (or dinner) are the meals that come later in the day when we get hungry again. The problem with this tack is that it ignores the social imperatives upon which it is based—imperatives which routinely place people who work odd hours or get hungry for the wrong things at the wrong times on the outside of the system as it is maintained. The fact that one may eat breakfast at two o'clock in the afternoon does not mean that one should. Missing meals does not mean losing weight; it means being separated from a customary event.

Appropriate eating includes not only eating the right things at the right times of day, but also observance of accepted practice in handling and consuming food. So it is that the parental admonishment "don't play with your food" echoes throughout American culture, distinguishing mealtimes as serious but social occasions. Creative eating tests these bounds, and what is regarded as natural and acceptable among children is seen as eccentric or psychotic among adults (hence the comic/horrific reaction around the dinner table to Richard Dreyfus's mashed potato model of Devil's Tower in the movie *Close Encounters of the Third Kind).* An Oreo cookie enjoyed filling first, or corn on the cob eaten in a purposeful vertical or horizontal pattern, represents individualistic, customary, creative acts made possible and tolerable by the

*It is as if, in a literal sense, our culture wishes to say that there is no difference between these two meals, but that breakfast, long the distant underdog among favored meals, is at the margins of social and culinary life. Calling it "the most important meal of the day" even further reduces the prospect of anyone's looking forward to it, and is about as positively persuasive as telling a child that of all the food on his plate the brussels sprouts are the best for him. If this is so, why would any restaurant want to serve breakfast all day?*

necessity of eating these foods with one's hands. Virtually all of the creative flourishes that embellish eating behavior are similar in this respect—the oyster tilted and slurped from its shell, an apple or orange carefully dissected, peeled grapes.

Some foods require a suspension of etiquette to be consumed—a breach of upbringing and decorum many eaters, including those with a taste for the food, cannot manage. Such is the case for steamed blue crabs, which turn hungry adults into mallet-wielding children whose pleasure derives as much from the mess that's made as from the small amount of meat extracted from the shells.

Instances of eating when one is not hungry might be termed nonnutritive uses of food, were it not for the fact that the sense of taste registers pleasure beyond the point of satiety. More specific examples of nonnutritive food use often approach play or sport, as in eating and drinking contests, or the consumption of foods for which taste is not the primary characteristic. Eating and drinking contests suspend the qualitative characteristics of the things being consumed—figuratively, by measuring the progress of contestants solely according to quantities consumed, and literally, by setting the goal of winning the contest above that of enjoying the food. The special cultural chemistry of these events includes a number of reversals—often employing foods that are particularly beloved for their taste but rendered tasteless to the contestants after the first few hurried portions, including pies, sausage, fried chicken, or oysters. One of the points of eating contests appears to be the inversion of the relationship between taste and appetite, attested by the frequent post mortem by contestants that they "never want to see another ———" as long as they live.

Foods that are eaten for nonnutritive effect also include prairie oysters or calf fries, as they are sometimes known—the cooked testes that are a byproduct of the annual branding, vaccinating, and castrating processes in cattle country, as well as other foods (or non-foods) eaten as a dare. Making it a matter of courage to eat something may or may not reflect the taste or other sensory characteristics of the thing being eaten—as proven by the number of first-time eaters of oysters (here referring to aquatic varieties) who are not comforted by the knowledge that the food they are about to eat is commonly enjoyed by great numbers of people.

There are also uses of food which are non-consumptive but perhaps unintentionally revealing of the associations of food and culture. Making things that aren't food out of foods or foodstuffs is often, but not always, associated with children, whose sense of the divisions between the cultural categories involved is not well developed. Virtually any food may serve as an effective projectile in a food fight, but among those more commonly packed in school lunches the piece of white bread distinguishes it-

*An Oreo cookie enjoyed filling first, or corn on the cob eaten in a purposeful vertical or horizontal pattern, represents individualistic, customary, creative acts made possible and tolerable by the necessity of eating these foods with one's hands. Virtually all of the creative flourishes that embellish eating behavior are similar in this respect—the oyster tilted and slurped from its shell, an apple or orange carefully dissected, peeled grapes.*

self. Sans crust, the bread can be compacted into a doughy ball about the size and weight of a shooting marble.

Decorated foods or foods used as decoration may test the sense of them as edible things. Easter eggs, of course, may be hard-boiled and edible, but an obvious investment of time and artistry may dissuade the recipient from eating it. Many ethnic groups respond to this dilemma by draining the raw egg from the shell before decorating it, thereby removing the object from the ranks of the edible. Among those that do not, the keeping of an elaborately decorated egg until its contents have dried and hardened is a task accorded some importance, since it is only after the egg is technically no longer edible that it wholly becomes a new and culturally distinct entity. Similarly, apples or other fruits given temporary faces or other costumes as holiday crafts may spend a brief time suspended between the categories of food and decor, where chocolate Easter rabbits also spend some brief time before their appeal as food surmounts their decorative attributes.

*Chef Jim Johnson puts the finishing touches on canapes artfully surrounding an ice sculpture. (Photo by Kay Danielson)*

# MARKING TIME: A HELIX OF CULTURE

Despite their variety and complexity, food events have a social and culinary language all their own. When we back away a bit from individual events, their similarities become apparent, types and patterns emerge, and cycles of repeated activities begin to take shape.

Cultural patterning of foodways may be found in the smallest details of events and customs—the regional preferences in turkey stuffing, the characteristic use of cinnamon in Greek-American cooking—as well as in the more pervasive and telling use of food in marking those occasions, ordinary and special, which measure the passage of time.

The first of these two kinds of patterning is the more common and stereotypical. It can be verified quantitatively, it is apparent to the senses, and it is culturally insignificant. Knowing that people in Iowa eat more potatoes than rice, and that people in South Carolina eat more rice than potatoes, uses social information to tell us about food. As anthropology, it does little more than enable us to call Iowans potato-eaters and South Carolinians rice-eaters—which is occasionally as much as we ask of the social sciences, and not altogether original, considering the popularity of similar food-based epithets used to deride nationality or regional groups. But in order to understand how food can tell us about people we must accept the fact that what they do with food is more revealing than the foods they do it with (or to).

The contexts for this kind of cultural measurement have a telescoping effect, offering particularity for observations made up-close, but significance that increases the farther back we stand. For foodways, the identification of the food event as the small-

*The world-famous Idaho potato goes to market. (Photo courtesy of Seaich Card & Souvenir Corporation)*

est significant unit is an argument about where we ought to stand in order to see what is culturally taking place. Whether or not you accept the argument, it follows that individual food events must be placed in an even larger context in order to be themselves understood. Some of the same prejudices that affect how we classify foods and meals come into play when we place a larger frame around food events. Barbecues tend to be compared just as barbecue is compared; a Greek-American wedding reception likened to an African-American wedding reception. The list of characteristics that barbecues have in common is short and varied, but still subject to disputation: meat cooked outdoors in fair weather, eaten outdoors by groups larger than a single household. Barbecues seem adaptable to political purposes, are often run by men, and are frequently fueled by beer, but as a type of event may range from a cookout involving a few next-door neighbors, where no particular food is actually called "barbecue," to large events whose culinary centerpiece and mainstay is barbecued meat, or meat turned by cookery into the thing named "barbecue." The barbecue universe is clearly distinguishable from the world of the birthday party or the wedding reception, yet its vocabulary is so hopelessly entangled (*barbecue* as a noun for the food and the food event, as a verb for the cooking process; *barbecued* as an adjective) that it requires broad mastery of culture and cookery to explain it.

I have maintained that there is a quantum difference between these levels of comparison, but if the true object of study is *how food means,* then increasingly longer strings of related events hold even greater revelations about people and how they use food to communicate their values. A wedding reception is a discrete (if complex) event within a period leading up to and surrounding the wedding that contains a

*Guests celebrate a Cambodian wedding with food and fellowship—an example of the food event expressing cultural identity. (Photo by Frank Proschan; courtesy of the American Folklife Center, Library of Congress)*

number of dinners, showers, and parties that are themselves individual, separable events but socially related to the larger purposes of the focal occasion. Comparing the way that Greek-American and African-American foodways are revealed in the sum of these wedding-related events would reveal much more than contrasting two receptions, not only because the culture-based details of the multiple events (menus, activities, etc.) would differ, but also because the number and kinds of events associated with a marriage in these communities would differ as well.

This is an important distinction, because it allows us to consider larger issues, such as the degree of formality that governs arrangements for this sort of event and the extent to which food is involved. The generous definition of a food event offered in Chapter Three includes occasions for which a fairly perfunctory offering of light food is a small part of the proceedings as well as affairs that are so largely dedicated to cooking or eating that other activities, if there are any, may appear totally incidental. The more elevated the grounds of comparison, however, the more useful it is to weigh the importance of food as an element in social proceedings. To return to the wedding example: a family or a community that eschews formal meetings to make arrangements, and favors talking about plans over dinner, is using food in a different way from one that prefers the more formal course. This characterization may be traced to ethnicity or other social variables, but a culture-based "way of doing things," or ethnomethodology, necessarily includes the full range of expressive forms through which that business is transacted—including the social use of food.

Strings of events that are connected by some pivotal occasion are only one of several larger units that prove useful in organizing individual food events. But a wedding is an event that takes place within a household only a few times, and its "specialness" in some ways begs the question raised earlier about reliance upon the atypical to explain the typical in culture. An event that requires a great deal of business may reveal much about how business is socially transacted, but do wedding arrangements reliably indicate how an annual Fourth of July picnic is organized?

In fact, what makes some occasions special may be the fact that they are marked for careful handling in comparison with more routine events—a distinction that may not be observed until the larger social cycle of food events, measured over a greater period of time than one special occasion per year or lifetime, is brought into the picture. With the lens opened this wide, the particulars of individual food events—the details inventoried via the descriptive outline—begin to blur, but the social life of a community and its use of food for marking time comes into focus. Stores closed so that families can be together for Thanksgiving; churches staking out dates for seasonal suppers to avoid splitting their following; hunting seasons and the freezer rentals they occasion—little parties and big celebrations cause a symbolic orchestration of food and social circumstance. A simple, chronological accounting for all food events within a calendar year would display a number of events, some circumscribed by occasions of individual importance, others experienced by greater numbers of community members irrespective of ethnic background, occupation, age, or other variables. If we look at the number of characteristics the people participating in a given event actually share, some categories emerge that prove useful in describing how food informs the cycles of community social life.

## EVENTS ASSOCIATED WITH COMMUNITY NATURAL CYCLE

Even today, those food events that are regulated by or celebrate changes in nature—the flow of maple sap, the migration of the grunion, the opening of oyster season, the emergence of the first greens of spring—continue to be most deeply rooted in community life, in part because they symbolically reflect nature's imprint upon human culture. Events that mark the harvest and the changing of seasons may not be among the more extravagant occasions in a year's social calendar, but they are the most widely felt and deeply rooted.

*Even today, those food events that are regulated by or celebrate changes in nature—the flow of maple sap, the migration of the grunion, the opening of oyster season, the emergence of the first greens of spring—continue to be most deeply rooted in community life, in part because they symbolically reflect nature's imprint upon human culture.*

In company towns, payday is everybody's harvest, and a company picnic is an event that celebrates community identity. In less homogenous circumstances, food events mark occasions of importance in the community economy, as the Florida rice pilau salutes the peanut crop that identifies and occupies a small town. Agricultural festivals, which tend toward a variety of activities that obscures the root reasons for their taking place, are not so much acts of homage to the crops or institutions that enable a community to survive, but occasions that bear the more subtle imprint of local economy. In contemporary America, the imprint may be of government, which contributes to the social calendar by releasing its employees on days that may have no other meaning to them but a work holiday. Having moved out from the common experience of nature to a more varied workplace, a community's economic cycle may not be all embracing, but it may mediate or affect most citizens.

America's cultural pluralism does not mitigate the presumption that the religious holidays celebrated by our forebears belong to all people, regardless of personal belief. The difficulties that non-Christians have in accommodating their religious holidays, and in making use of the shut-down time officially provided for Easter and Christmas, clearly illustrate the conflicts inherent in a religious cycle that *is* culturally exclusive, and the importance of thinking of a community's religious calendar and its attendant foodways in the plural. The account of an all-day preaching and dinner-on-the-grounds from Alabama that appears in Chapter Three describes the entire population of the community where the event occurs as belonging to one of two churches—one Baptist, the other Methodist—built side-by-side and sharing in an annual event where ***non-denominational*** Christian fellowship was enjoyed. This event, and others like it—camp meetings, cemetery cleanings, church anniversaries, Christmas caroling parties—are part of a cycle of annual and occasional food events that marks religious time. In lower Talledega county, in 1941, most of this calendar was as deeply rooted and widely shared as the changing of the seasons; in modern America, a community's religious cycle is generally culturally fixed, but less "elective" than the social cycle described below.

Those occasions that bring a community together on grounds other than common experience of the season, local economy, and religion may seem more culturally splintered, but account for the majority of a year's food events and celebratory calendar. Some affect more people than others; some respect ethnic, age, or family lines, but many cross over them in ways that define an individual community as a product of its own particular history, traditions, and civic temperament. These occasions include such varied food events as parties that mark the last day of the school year, family reunions, the banquets of clubs and societies, fundraisers for athletic teams, teen dances, and church suppers. It is interesting to note that different people experience these occasions in different ways—not necessarily as members of the group circumscribed by an event. For example, some Jewish families use the government and school holidays for Christmas as an opportunity to schedule family reunions, knowing that the chances for family members to get away from work or classes on those

*Melons, peaches, and fish are all among seasonal foodstuffs that shape the annual cycle of food events in a community. (Photo by Walker Evans; courtesy of the FSA Collection, Library of Congress)*

days are better than average. Get-togethers for parents of preschool children are often parallel events created by the circumstance of organizing parties for the youngsters.[1]

Looking at the different cycles of food events within a given community in terms of their degree of commonality and cultural imprint also provides the means to describe how a particular event—or its community significance—may change over time. The ability of modern food processing technology, for example, to make supplies of virtually any foodstuff available anywhere in the country year-round affects the *real* anticipation with which spring produce, including greens, may be awaited, and gradually diminishes the importance of occasions that mark the beginning of a new season with events involving such foods. Some events of the past have been stymied by technological change. Threshers' or sheepshearers' dinners, for example, were based upon a system of cooperative use of threshing equipment and crews of itinerant shearers, moved farm to farm during the appropriate season. But because farm-owned combines have replaced threshers, and hand shears have been replaced by electric ones, threshers' dinners in some communities have shifted from "real" to symbolic events. They continue to take place as fulfillment of a social, rather than a technological, imperative.

Changes in the technology of farm life did not themselves represent a threat to threshers' or sheepshearers' *suppers,* but changes in rural cultures affected by these innovations affect the entire cycle of economic life. As a result, changes that affect the natural or economic cycles within a community are likely to force food events associated with those cycles into the social cycle. Similarly, it is rare that an invented occasion, like a newly declared state or federal holiday, will generate food events that penetrate the cycles more central to community life than the social cycle. This does not mean that patterns of food events are the inevitable victims of technological or social change, but that the bases for adherence to them tend to become increasingly voluntary and bear a less recognizable relationship to natural cycles. In this sense, foodways increasingly becomes the property of ever-smaller groups and a much less accurate reflection of indigenous (i.e., "natural") social patterns.

Just as importantly, however, this view of food and culture, seen through traditional ways of marking time, brings us closer to understanding a culture's generative abilities—not just the template that creates statements according to a given custom, but how tradition adapts to changing circumstances—a city neighborhood whose block party now must reach out to recently arrived neighbors from faraway places; the marking of an event, like the anniversary of Columbus's voyages to the Americas, or the turn of the century, that has ethnic as well as national historical significance, yet which is celebrated only once every hundred years.

Here, in fact, is where the notion of cycles fails us, since the ability to create new events or change them does not derive from the experience of an annually repeated series of occasions and their customary observance in food and activity, but from their cumulative effect. People do not simply create events to compensate for such social dislocations as moving to a new place, the diffusion of a formerly close-knit family, or a change in religious values. In fact, many strive to wrench these realities into alignment with a social order to which they have become accustomed—staying put when opportunities to move on may beckon, driving great distances to reunite with family members at customary reunion times, or remaining a member of a congregation for social, if not spiritual, fulfillment. Our reasons for these attachments are more deeply rooted than the events which are their symbols. Nobody would admit to remaining a member of a church simply because he or she loved its suppers, but subtract the capability to merge fellowship and sustenance in a ham and oyster supper and a congregation is impoverished in its ability to serve its members as whole people. Food may not be the first thing that comes to mind when a tour of duty or job transfer takes a family member away from kin for a year, but it is through recalling Sunday dinners and Fourth of July barbecues that this loss is often measured.

Foodways in America is a helix of events, a coiling or intertwining of the strands of our very identity. The strands vary with time and yet maintain consistency. Each school picnic is the same, but each picnicker is different—a sixth-grader now, and no longer a fifth-. Each family Thanksgiving dinner is another turkey, and perhaps—joyfully—another mouth to feed, or—sadly—one less. In an ascending spiral that grasps the familiar for a sense of history and direction, the events that compose a common and varied culture are the truest reflection of what we value most.

*People do not simply create events to compensate for such social dislocations as moving to a new place, the diffusion of a formerly close-knit family, or a change in religious values. In fact, many strive to wrench these realities into alignment with a social order to which they have become accustomed—staying put when opportunities to move on may beckon, driving great distances to reunite with family members at customary reunion times, or remaining a member of a congregation for social, if not spiritual, fulfillment. Our reasons for these attachments are more deeply rooted than the events which are their symbols. Nobody would admit to remaining a member of a church simply because he or she loved its suppers, but subtract the capability to merge fellowship and sustenance in a ham and oyster supper and a congregation is impoverished in its ability to serve its members as whole people. Food may not be the first thing that comes to mind when a tour of duty or job transfer takes a family member away from kin for a year, but it is through recalling Sunday dinners and Fourth of July barbecues that this loss is often measured.*

# NOTES

All references to the America Eats manuscript collection are abbreviated as follows: AE (America Eats) followed by a two-letter code for the state or regional file in which cited material is located, followed by the number of the essay within a state or regional file, followed by the page on which the material appears within the essay. The America Eats manuscript collection was gathered and partially prepared for publication by the U.S. Government's Works Progress Administration, Federal Writers' Program, between 1939 and 1941. The collection is housed in the Manuscript Division of the Library of Congress.

## Chapter One. AN OVERVIEW

[1] Carl E. Guthe, memorandum "Food and Folkways," November 21, 1943, pp. 3-4, National Research Council Committee on Food Habits files, Washington, D.C.

[2] Dorothy Dickins, *Occupations of Sons and Daughters of Mississippi Cotton Farmers* (Ph.D. dissertation, University of Chicago, 1937). See also Dorothy Dickins, Day Monroe, and Pearl Greene, "Research in Family Economics," *Journal of Home Economics* 36.8 (October 1944).

## Chapter Two. FOODWAYS AND AMERICAN FOLKLIFE

[1] AEMW 1, p. 48.

[2] AEVT 2, pp. 6-7.

[3] AEGA 1, p. 7.

[4] AESO 14, p. 45.

[5] AEOK 9, p. 1.

[6] AETX 5, p. 6.

[7] AEWY 1, p. 3.

[8] AEUT 1, p. 12.

[9] AESO 5, p. 13.

[10] AEWA 7, p. 1.

[11] See Jan Brunvand, *The Vanishing Hitchhiker* (New York: W.W. Norton & Co., 1981); *The Choking Doberman* (New York: W.W. Norton & Co., 1984); and *The Mexican Pet* (New York: W.W. Norton & Co., 1986).

[12] AEFW 1, p. 21.

[13] AEFW 1, p. 26.

[14] AECO 27, p. 1.

[15] Hans Kurath, *A Word Geography of the Eastern United States* (Ann Arbor, Michigan: University of Michigan Press, 1970), pp. 67-69.

[16] AEAR 2, pp. 1-2.

[17] AEWY 1, p. 5.

[18] AESC 2, p. 3.

[19] AEAL 2, p. 3.

[20] AEMW 1, p. 7.

[21] AEMW 1, p. 12.

[22] AEMW 1, p. 13.

[23] AEMW 1, p. 19.

[24] AEMW 1, p. 22.

[25] AEMW 1, p. 21.

[26] AEMS 17, p. 1.

[27] AESO 1, p. 2.

[28] AESO 6, p. 18.

[29] Roland Freeman, *The Arabbers of Baltimore* (Cambridge, Maryland: Tidewater Press, 1989).

[30] AEMD 1, pp. 5-6.

[31] AEMD 1, p. 6.

[32] Recorded by Michael Tiranoff for the film *Arabbin'* (Winchester, Massachusetts: Brainstorm Films, 1976).

[33] AESO 1, p. 2.

[34] AESO 1, p. 2.

[35] AESO 7, p. 1.

[36] AESO 14, p. 1.

[37] See George Carey, *A Faraway Time and Place* (Washington and New York: Robert B. Luce, 1971) and Patrick B. Mullen, *I Heard the Old Fisherman Say* (Austin: University of Texas Press, 1978).

[38]AESC 13, p. 2; and AEVA 14, p. 2.

[39]AEMW 1, pp. 49-50.

[40]AESW 1, p. 24.

[41]AEUT 1, pp. 17-18.

[42]AEOR 1, p. 1.

[43]See Robert W. McCarl, *The District of Columbia Fire Fighters' Project: A Case Study in Occupational Folklife* (Washington: Smithsonian Institution Press, 1985; Smithsonian Folklife Studies Number 4), especially pp. 57-61.

[44]AEOR 4, p. 3.

[45]AEFL 6, p. 1.

[46]Kathy Neustadt, "Born Among the Shells: The Quakers of Allen's Neck and Their Clambake," in Theodore C. Humphrey and Lin T. Humphrey, eds., *"We Gather Together": Food and Festival in American Life* (Ann Arbor, Michigan: UMI Research Press, 1988), pp. 89-109.

[47]For non-recipe examples of Xerox-lore, see Alan Dundes and Carl R. Pagter, *Urban Folklore from the Paperwork Empire* (Austin, Texas: American Folklore Society, PAFS 62, 1965).

[48]AENB 1, pp. 3-4.

[49]AENB 32, p. 1.

[50]See Christina Hardyment, *From Mangle to Microwave: The Mechanization of Household Work* (Cambridge and New York: Polity Press and Basil Blackwell, Inc., 1988).

## Chapter Three. THE FOOD EVENT

[1]See Charles Camp, "Foodways in Everyday Life," *American Quarterly* 34.3 (Bibliography, 1982): 278-89.

[2]AEAL 3.

[3]AEFL 1. Written by Stetson Kennedy.

[4]AEIO 9.

[5]AENB 18. Written by Lovica Langley.

[6]AENB 26.1

## Chapter Four. FROM FIELD TO TABLE

[1]See especially Mary Douglas, "The Abominations of Leviticus," in her *Purity and Danger* (New York: Praeger Books, 1966), pp. 41-57.

[2]Dorothy Dickins, "Geophagy among Mississippi Negro School Children," *American Sociological Review* 7 (February 1942): 59-65.

[3]See Alice Shorett and Murray Morgan, *The Pike Place Market: People, Politics, and Produce* (Seattle, Washington: Pacific Search Press, 1982), and John Stamets, *Portrait of a Market: Photographs of Seattle's Pike Place Market* (Seattle, Washington: Real Comet Press, 1987).

[4]Federal Writers' Project, Works Progress Administration, *U.S. One: Maine to Florida* (New York: Modern Age Books, 1938).

[5]*U.S. One*, p. xxvii.

[6]Federal Writers' Project, Works Progress Administration, *The Ocean Highway: New Brunswick, New Jersey to Jacksonville, Florida* (New York, Modern Age Books, 1938), p. xxiii.

[7]Thomas A. Adler, "Making Pancakes on Sunday: The Male Cook in Family Tradition," *Western Folklore* 40.1 (January 1981): 45-54.

[8]Claude Lévi-Strauss, "The Roast and the Boiled," in Jessica Kuper, ed., *The Anthropologists' Cookbook* (New York: Universe Books, 1977), pp. 221-30.

[9]See Timothy C. Lloyd, "The Cincinnati Chili Culinary Complex," *Western Folklore* 40.1 (January 1981): 28-40.

[10]Ibid.

[11]See, for example, Robert Opie, *The Art of the Label: Designs of the Times* (Secaucus, New Jersey: Chartwell Books, 1987), and Kay and Marsha Lee, eds., *America's Favorites* (New York: G.P. Putnam & Sons, 1980).

[12]See Harvey Levenstein, *Revolution at the Table: The Transformation of the American Diet* (New York: Oxford University Press, 1988).

[13]Amy Shuman, "The Rhetoric of Portions," *Western Folklore* 40.1 (January 1981): 72-80.

## Chapter Five. MARKING TIME: THE HELIX OF CULTURE

[1]See Nancy Klavans, "A Halloween Brunch: The Affirmation of Group in a Temporary Community," in Theodore C. and Lin T. Humphrey, eds., *"We Gather Together": Food and Festival in American Life* (Ann Arbor, Michigan: UMI Research Press, 1988), p. 43-50.

# BIBLIOGRAPHY

## BOOKS AND ARTICLES

Adler, Thomas A. "Making Pancakes on Sunday: The Male Cook in Family Tradition." *Western Folklore* 40.1 (January 1981): 45–54.

*The American Heritage Cookbook and Illustrated History of American Eating and Drinking.* New York: American Heritage Publishing, 1964.

Anderson, Jay Allan. "Scholarship on Contemporary American Folk Foodways." *Ethnologia Europaea* 5 (1971): 56–63.

Andrews, Jean. *Peppers: The Domesticated Capsicums.* Austin: University of Texas Press, 1984.

Arnott, Margaret L., ed. *Gastronomy: The Anthropology of Food and Food Habits.* The Hague: Mouton Publishers, 1975.

Barber, Edith M. "The Development of the American Food Pattern." *Journal of the American Dietetic Association* 24 (July 1948): 586–91.

Barthes, Roland. "Ornamental Cookery." In his *Mythologies.* Paris: Editions du Seuil, 1957, pp. 78–80.

———. "Toward a Psychosociology of Contemporary Food Consumption." In Elborg Forster and Robert Forster, eds., *European Diet from Pre-Industrial to Modern Times.* New York: Harper & Row, 1975, pp. 47–59.

Beard, James A. *James Beard's American Cookery.* Boston: Little, Brown, 1972.

Bennett, John. "Food and Culture in Southern Illinois." *American Sociological Review* 7 (October 1942): 645–60.

———. "An Interpretation of the Scope and Implications of Social Scientific Research in Human Subsistence." *American Anthropologist* 48 (October 1946): 553–73.

Biester, Charlotte Elizabeth. *Some Factors in the Development of American Cookbooks.* Field Study Number 2. Ann Arbor, Michigan: University Microfilms, 1950.

Bourke, John Gregory. "The Folk Foods of the Rio Grande Valley and of Northern Mexico." *Journal of American Folklore* 8 (January–March, 1895): 41–71.

Brown, Bob, and Eleanor Parker. *Culinary Americana: 1860–1960.* New York: Roving Eye Press, 1961.

Brown, Dale. *American Cooking.* New York: Time, Inc., 1968.

———. *American Cooking: The Northwest.* New York: Time, Inc., 1970.

Brown, Linda Keller, and Kay Mussell, eds. *Ethnic and Regional Foodways in the United States: The Performance of Group Identity.* Knoxville: University of Tennessee Press, 1984.

Burton, Thomas G., and Ambrose N. Manning. "Folk Methods of Preserving and Processing Food." East Tennessee University Monograph Series, no. 3. Johnson City, Tennessee: Institute of Regional Studies, 1966, pp. 27–31.

Camp, Charles. "Foodways in Everyday Life." *American Quarterly* 34.3 (Bibliography, 1982): 278–89.

———. "Food in American Culture: A Bibliographic Essay." *Journal of American Culture* 2.3 (Fall, 1979): 559–70.

Carson, Jane. *Colonial Virginia Cookery.* Williamsburg, Virginia: Colonial Williamsburg, Inc., 1968.

Cassell, B. "Jewish Dietary Laws and Food Customs." *Public Health Nursing* 32 (November 1940): 685–87.

Chang, B. "Some Dietary Beliefs in Chinese Folk Culture." *Journal of the American Dietetic Association* 65 (October 1974): 436–38.

Claiborne, Craig. *The New York Times Guide to Dining Out in New York.* Rev. ed. New York: Atheneum, 1968.

Clark, Faith, ed. *Symposium III: The Changing Patterns of Consumption of Food.* International Congress of Food Science and Technology. Proceedings of the Congress Symposia, 1962. Volume 5. New York: Gordon and Breach Science Publications, 1967, pp. 159–254.

Collin, Richard. *New Orleans Underground Gourmet.* New York: Simon and Schuster, 1973.

———. *New Orleans Restaurant Guide.* New Orleans: Strether and Swann, 1977.

———. *The Pleasures of Seafood.* New York: Holt, Rinehart, and Winston, 1977.

Committee on Food Habits, National Research Council. *The Problem of Changing Food Habits.* Bulletin of the National Research Council 108, October 1943. Washington, D.C.: National Research Council, 1943.

———. *Manual for the Study of Food Habits.* Bulletin of the National Research Council 111, January 1945. Washington, D.C.: National Research Council, 1945.

Cummings, Richard Osborn. *The American and his Food: A History of Food Habits in the United States.* Chicago: University of Chicago Press, 1940.

Cussler, Margaret, and Mary Louise de Give. *Twixt the Cup and the Lip: Psychological and Socio-Cultural Factors Affecting Food Habits*. New York: Twayne Publishers, 1952.

Dickins, Dorothy. "Food Preparation of Owner and Cropper Farm Families in the Shortleaf Pine Area of Mississippi." *Social Forces* 22 (October 1943): 56–63.

————. "Changing Pattern of Food Preparation of Small Town Families in Mississippi." Mississippi Agricultural Experimental Station *Bulletin* 415 (1945): 1–56.

————and R.N. Ford. "Geophagy among Mississippi Negro School Children." *American Sociological Review* 7 (February 1942): 59–65.

Dickson, Paul. *Chow: A Cook's Tour of Military Food*. New York: New American Library, 1978.

Dodson, R. "Tortilla Making." In *In the Shadow of History*, Texas Folklore Society Publications 15 (1939), pp. 1–18.

Douglas, Mary. "The Abominations of Leviticus." In her *Purity and Danger*. New York: Praeger Books, 1966, pp. 41–57.

————. "Deciphering a Meal." In Clifford Geertz, ed., *Myth, Symbol, and Culture*. New York: W.W. Norton, 1971, pp. 61–81.

————, ed., *Food in the Social Order: Studies of Food and Festivities in Three American Communities*. New York: Russell Sage Foundation, 1984.

Feibleman, Peter S., and the Editors of Time-Life Books. *American Cooking: Creole and Acadian*. New York: Time, Inc., 1971.

Glaser, Milton, and Jerome Snyder. *The Underground Gourmet*. Rev. ed. New York: Simon and Schuster, 1970.

Greene, Gael. *Bite*. New York: W.W. Norton, 1971.

Hardyment, Christina. *From Mangle to Microwave: The Mechanization of Household Work*. Cambridge and New York: Polity Press and Basil Blackwell, Inc., 1988.

Harris, Marvin. *Cows, Pigs, Wars, and Witches: The Riddles of Culture*. New York: Random House, 1974.

————. *Good to Eat: Riddles of Food and Culture*. New York: Simon and Schuster, 1985.

Hirshorn, Paul, and Steven Izenour. *White Towers*. Cambridge: Massachusetts Institute of Technology Press, 1979.

Humphrey, N.D. "Some Dietary and Health Practices of Detroit Mexicans." *Journal of American Folklore* 58 (July 1945): 255–58.

Humphrey, Theodore C., and Lin T. Humphrey, eds. *"We Gather Together": Food and Festivity in American Life*. Ann Arbor, Michigan: UMI Research Press, 1988.

Jones, Michael Owens, Bruce Giuliano, and Roberta Krell, eds. *Foodways and Eating Habits: Directions for Research*. Los Angeles: California Folklore Society, 1981.

Jordan, G.L. *Changing Food Habits in Relation to Land Utilization in the United States*. Carbondale: University of Illinois Press, 1933.

Klavans, Nancy. "A Halloween Brunch: The Affirmation of Group in a Temporary Community." In Theodore C. and Lin T. Humphrey, eds., *"We Gather Together": Food and Festivity in American Life*. Ann Arbor, Michigan: UMI Research Press, 1988, pp. 43–50.

Kroc, Ray. *Grinding It Out: The Making of McDonald's*. Chicago: Henry Regnery, 1977.

Langdon, Philip. *Orange Roofs, Golden Arches: The Architecture of American Chain Restaurants*. New York: Alfred A. Knopf, 1986.

Lasky, Michael S. *The Complete Junk Food Book*. New York: McGraw-Hill, 1977.

Leach, Edmund. "Cooking." In his *Culture and Communication*. New York: Cambridge University Press, 1976, pp. 60–61.

Lee, Kay and Marshall, eds. *America's Favorites*. New York: G.P. Putnam's Sons, 1980.

Le Gros, Clark F. "Human Food Habits as Determining the Basic Patterns of Economic and Social Life." *Nutrition* 22 (January 1966): 134–45.

Leonard, Jonathan Norton, and the Editors of Time-Life Books. *American Cooking: New England*. New York: Time, Inc., 1970.

————. *American Cooking: The Great West*. New York: Time, Inc., 1971.

Levenstein, Harvey. *Revolution at the Table: The Transformation of the American Diet*. New York: Oxford University Press, 1988.

Lévi-Strauss, Claude. "The Culinary Triangle." *Partisan Review* 33 (Fall 1966): 586–95.

————. "The Roast and the Boiled." In Jessica Kuper, ed. *The Anthropologists' Cookbook*. New York: Universe Books, 1977, pp. 221–30.

Lincoln, Waldo. *American Cookery Books, 1742*–1860. Worcester, Massachusetts: American Antiquarian Society, 1954.

Lloyd, Timothy C. "The Cincinnati Chili Culinary Complex." *Western Folklore* 40.1 (January 1981): 28–40.

Loeb, M.B. "The Social Functions of Food Habits." *Journal of Applied Nutrition* 4 (1951): 227–29.

Lowenberg, M.E. "Socio-Cultural Basis of Food Habits." *Food Technology* 24 (1970): 27–32.

Massachusetts State Department of Health. *The Food of Working Women in Boston.* Studies in Economic Relations of Women, vol. 10. Boston: Women's Educational and Industrial Union, Department of Research, 1917.

Mead, Margaret. "Dietary Patterns and Food Habits." *Journal of the American Dietetic Association* 19 (January 1943): 1–5.

———. "The Challenge of Cross-Cultural Research." *Journal of the American Dietetic Association* 45 (December 1964): 413–14.

———. *Food Habits Research: Problems of the 1960s.* Washington, D.C.: National Research Council publication 1225, 1964.

Mickler, Ernest Matthew. *Sinkin Spells, Hot Flashes, Fits and Cravins.* Berkeley, California: Ten Speed Press, 1988.

Moser, Ada M. *Farm Family Diets in the Lower Coastal Plains of South Carolina.* South Carolina Agricultural Experimental Station Bulletin 319, 1939.

———. *Food Habits of South Carolina Farm Families.* South Carolina Agricultural Experimental Station Bulletin 343, 1942.

Neustadt, Kathy. "Born Among the Shells: The Quakers of Allen's Neck and their Clambake." In Theodore C. and Lin T. Humphrey, eds. *"We Gather Together": Food and Festival in American Life.* Ann Arbor, Michigan: UMI Research Press, 1988, pp. 89–109.

Newall, Venetia. "Selected Jamaican Foodways in Homeland and in England." In Linda Dégh, Henry Glassie, and Felix J. Oinas, eds., *Folklore Today.* Bloomington: Indiana University Press, 1976, pp. 369–77.

Niehoff, Arthur H. "Food Habits and Cultural Patterns." In The Nutrition Foundation, Inc., *Food Science and Society.* New York: The Nutrition Foundation, 1969, pp. 45–52.

Opie, Robert. *The Art of the Label.* Secaucus, New Jersey: Chartwell Books, 1987.

Patten, Marguerite. *Books for Cooks: Bibliography of Cookery.* N.p., 1975.

Paz, Octavio. "Eroticism and Gastrostrophy." *Daedalus* 101 (Fall 1972): 67–85.

Phillips, Doris E., and Mary A. Bass. "Food Preservation Practices of Selected Homemakers in East Tennessee." *Ecology of Food and Nutrition* 5 (Winter 1976): 26–39.

Pyke, Magnus. *Food and Society.* London: John Murray, 1968.

———. "The Influence of American Foods and Food Technology in Europe." In C.W.E. Bigsby, ed., *Superculture: American Popular Culture and Europe.* Bowling Green, Ohio: Bowling Green University Popular Press, 1975, pp. 83–95.

Read, R.B. *The San Francisco Underground Gourmet.* New York: Simon and Schuster, 1969.

Root, Waverly. *The Food of France.* New York: Alfred A. Knopf, 1958.

——— and Richard de Rochement. *Eating in America: A History.* New York: William Morrow, 1976.

Sackett, Marjorie. "Folk Recipes as a Measure of Intercultural Penetration." *Journal of American Folklore* 85 (January–March 1972): 77–91.

Sakr, A.H. "Dietary Regulations and Food Habits of Muslims." *Journal of the American Dietetic Association* 58 (February 1971): 123–26.

Schweid, Richard. *Hot Peppers: Cajuns and Capsicum in New Iberia, Louisiana.* Seattle, Washington: Madrona Publishers, 1980.

Shapiro, Laura. *Perfection Salad: Women and Cooking at the Turn of the Century.* New York: Farrar, Straus, and Giroux, 1986.

Shenton, James Patrick, et al. *American Cooking: The Melting Pot.* New York: Time, Inc., 1971.

Shorett, Alice, and Murray Morgan. *The Pike Place Market: People, Politics, and Produce.* Seattle, Washington: Pacific Search Press, 1982.

Shuman, Amy. "The Rhetoric of Portions." *Western Folklore* 40.1 (January 1981): 72–80.

Sokolov, Raymond. *Fading Feast: A Compendium of Disappearing American Regional Foods.* New York: Farrar, Straus, and Giroux, 1981.

Sorre, Max. "The Geography of Diet." In Phillip L. Wagner and Marvin W. Mikesell, eds., *Readings in Cultural Geography.* Chicago: University of Chicago Press, 1962, pp. 445–56.

Stamets, John. *Portrait of a Market: Photographs of Seattle's Pike Place Market.* Seattle, Washington: Real Comet Press, 1987.

Steinberg, Sally Levitt. *The Donut Book.* New York: Alfred A. Knopf, 1987.

Stern, Jane, and Michael Stern. *Roadfood.* New York: Random House, 1977.

———. *A Taste of America.* Kansas City and New York: Andrews and McKeel, 1988.

Todhunter, E.N. "The History of Food Patterns in the U.S.A." In *Proceedings of the Third International Congress on Dietetics.* New York: The Nutrition Foundation, 1961.

Trillin, Calvin. *Third Helpings.* New Haven and New York: Ticknor & Fields, 1983.

———. *American Fried.* New York: Penguin Books, 1975.

———. *Alice, Let's Eat.* New York: Random House, 1978. U.S. Department of Agriculture. *Experimental Station Record.* Washington, D.C.: United States Department of Agriculture, 1889–.

U.S. Department of Health, Education, and Welfare. *Cumulated Index Medicus.* Washington, D.C.: National Institutes of Health, Public Health Service, 1959–.

Vance, Rupert B. "Climate, Diet, and Human Adequacy." In his *Human Geography of the South.* Chapel Hill: University of North Carolina Press, 1932, pp. 411–41.

Vehling, Joseph Dommers. *America's Table.* Chicago: Hostends, 1950.

Vennum, Thomas Jr. *Wild Rice and the Ojibway People.* St. Paul: Minnesota Historical Society Press, 1988.

Viorst, Judith, and Milton Viorst. *The Washington, DC, Underground Gourmet.* New York: Simon and Schuster, 1970.

Walter, Eugene. *American Cooking: Southern Style.* New York: Time, Inc., 1971.

Weaver, William Woys, ed. *A Quaker Woman's Cookbook: The Domestic Cookery of Elizabeth Ellicott Lea.* Philadelphia: University of Pennsylvania Press, 1982.

Welsch, Roger. "We Are What We Eat: Omaha Food as Symbol." *Keystone Folklore Quarterly* 16 (Winter 1971): 165–70.

Wilson, Christine S. "Food Habits: A Selected Annotated Bibliography." *Journal of Nutrition Education* 5 (January–March 1973): supplement 1, 36–72.

Wilson, José. *American Cooking: The Eastern Heartland.* New York: Time, Inc., 1971.

Yoder, Don. "Sauerkraut in the Pennsylvania Folk Culture." *Pennsylvania Folklife* 12 (Summer 1961): 56–59.

———. "Schnitz in the Pennsylvania Folk Culture." *Pennsylvania Folklife* 12 (Fall 1961), 56–59.

———. "Historical Sources for American Foodways Research and Plans for an American Foodways Archive." *Pennsylvania Folklife* 20 (Spring 1971): 16–29.

———. "Folk Cookery." In Richard M. Dorson, ed., *Folklore and Folklife: An Introduction.* Chicago: University of Chicago Press, 1972, pp. 325–50.

## PERIODICALS

*The Digest.* Philadelphia, Pennsylvania, 1977–.

*Ecology of Food and Nutrition.* London, 1971–.

*Food and Foodways.* London, 1986–.

*International Review of Food and Wine.* New York, 1958–.

*Journal of the American Dietetic Association.* Chicago, 1925–.

*Journal of Nutrition Education.* Berkeley, California, 1969–.

*Natural History.* New York, 1900–.

*Nutrition Abstracts and Reviews.* Boston, 1942–.